WRITTEN BY *Brad Timm*   ILLUSTRATED BY *Jill De Haan*
AND *Margaux Samson Abadie*

America is Wild!

A STATE-BY-STATE ENCYCLOPEDIA OF AMERICAN WILDLIFE

WIDE EYED EDITIONS

CONTENTS

3	INTRODUCTION
4-7	ALABAMA
8-11	ALASKA
12-15	ARIZONA
16-19	ARKANSAS
20-23	CALIFORNIA
24-27	COLORADO
28-31	CONNECTICUT
32-35	DELAWARE
36-39	FLORIDA
40-43	GEORGIA
44-47	HAWAII
48-51	IDAHO
52-55	ILLINOIS
56-59	INDIANA
60-63	IOWA
64-67	KANSAS
68-71	KENTUCKY
72-75	LOUISIANA
76-79	MAINE
80-83	MARYLAND
84-87	MASSACHUSETTS
88-91	MICHIGAN
92-95	MINNESOTA
96-99	MISSISSIPPI
100-103	MISSOURI
104-107	MONTANA
108-111	NEBRASKA
112-115	NEVADA
116-119	NEW HAMPSHIRE
120-123	NEW JERSEY
124-127	NEW MEXICO
128-131	NEW YORK
132-135	NORTH CAROLINA
136-139	NORTH DAKOTA
140-143	OHIO
144-147	OKLAHOMA
148-151	OREGON
152-155	PENNSYLVANIA
156-159	RHODE ISLAND
160-163	SOUTH CAROLINA
164-167	SOUTH DAKOTA
168-171	TENNESSEE
172-175	TEXAS
176-179	UTAH
180-183	VERMONT
184-187	VIRGINIA
188-191	WASHINGTON
192-195	WEST VIRGINIA
196-199	WISCONSIN
200-203	WYOMING
204-207	INDEX

INTRODUCTION FROM THE AUTHOR

THE UNITED STATES CONTAINS AN AMAZING DIVERSITY OF ANIMALS, FROM TINY CREATURES LIKE ANTS AND BEETLES TO HUGE ONES, LIKE GRIZZLY BEARS AND BISON. The variety of plants you'll find in the U.S. is even greater—ranging from delicate wildflowers all the way up to the 640-ton giant sequoia trees of California!

America Is Wild! features nearly 200 animals and 200 plants found in the U.S. For each of the fifty states, it showcases four of the most common or characteristic animal and plant species. You can tell a lot about a place by the things that thrive there. For example, the animals and plants chosen for Arizona are all well adapted to living in desert climates. By contrast, those selected for Alaska are those that can survive in freezing conditions.

For each state featured in this book, you will usually find one of each of the following: a mammal, a bird, an amphibian or reptile, and an insect or invertebrate. Similarly, the four plants selected for each state generally include a mix of trees, shrubs, fruits, wildflowers, and herbaceous plants.

While you won't find every animal and plant in the U.S. in *America is Wild!*, you will get a very good idea of the country's wildlife and plants. You'll certainly get acquainted with some of the most iconic species, and in the process get better acquainted with the U.S.A. itself!

HOW TO USE THIS BOOK

STATE HEADER: A brief overview of each state, including a general description of the habitats found there and a measure of the number of the animals and plants present

COMMON NAME: The name used by most people when referring to the animal or plant

LATIN NAME: The scientific, Latin name for the animal or plant, used all over the world, no matter what language is spoken

FACT FILE: Interesting facts about each animal or plant

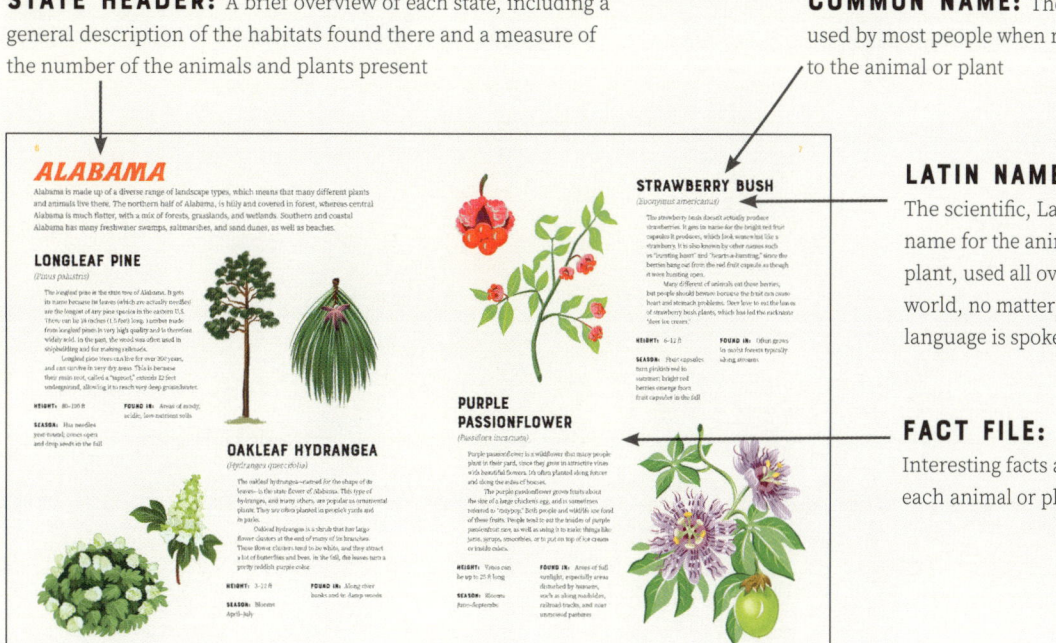

ALABAMA

Alabama is made up of a diverse range of landscape types, which means that many different plants and animals live there. The northern half of Alabama is hilly and covered in forest, whereas central Alabama is much flatter, with a mix of forests, grasslands, and wetlands. Southern and coastal Alabama has many freshwater swamps, saltmarshes, and sand dunes, as well as beaches.

LONGLEAF PINE
(Pinus palustris)

The longleaf pine is the state tree of Alabama. It gets its name because its leaves (which are actually needles) are the longest of any pine species in the eastern U.S. These can be 18 inches (1.5 feet) long. Lumber made from longleaf pines is very high quality and is therefore widely sold. In the past, the wood was often used in shipbuilding and for making railroads.

Longleaf pine trees can live for over 300 years and can survive in very dry areas. This is because their main root, called a "taproot," extends 12 feet underground, allowing it to reach very deep groundwater.

HEIGHT: 80–100 ft.

FOUND IN: Areas of sandy, acidic, low-nutrient soils

SEASON: Has needles year-round; cones open and drop their seeds in the fall

OAKLEAF HYDRANGEA
(Hydrangea quercifolia)

The oakleaf hydrangea—named for the shape of its leaves—is the state flower of Alabama. This type of hydrangea, and many others, are popular as ornamental plants. They are often planted in people's yards and in parks.

Oakleaf hydrangea is a shrub that has large flower clusters at the end of many of its branches. These flower clusters tend to be white, and they attract a lot of butterflies and bees. In the fall, the leaves turn a pretty reddish-purple color.

HEIGHT: 3–12 ft.

FOUND IN: Along riverbanks and in damp woods

SEASON: Blooms April–July

STRAWBERRY BUSH
(Euonymus americanus)

The strawberry bush doesn't actually produce strawberries. It gets its name for the bright-red fruit capsules it produces, which look somewhat like strawberries. It is also known by other names such as "bursting heart" and "hearts-a-bursting," since the berries hang out from the red fruit capsules as though they were bursting open.

Many different animals eat these berries, but people should beware because the fruit can cause heart and stomach problems. Deer love to eat the leaves of strawberry bush plants, which has led to the nickname "deer ice cream."

HEIGHT: 6–12 ft.

SEASON: Fruit capsules turn pinkish red in summer; bright-red berries emerge from fruit capsules in the fall

FOUND IN: Often grows in moist forests, typically along streams

PURPLE PASSIONFLOWER
(Passiflora incarnata)

Purple passionflower is a wildflower that many people plant in their yards, since it grows in attractive vines with beautiful flowers. It's often planted along fences and along the sides of houses.

The purple passionflower grows fruits about the size of a large chicken's egg, and is sometimes referred to as "maypop." Both people and wildlife are fond of these fruits. People tend to eat the insides of purple passionfruit raw, as well as using it to make things like jelly, syrups, and smoothies, or to put on top of ice cream or inside cakes.

HEIGHT: Vines can be up to 25 ft. long

SEASON: Blooms June–September

FOUND IN: Areas of full sunlight, especially areas disturbed by humans, such as along roadsides, railroad tracks, and near unmowed pastures

ALABAMA

AMERICAN BEAVER
(Castor canadensis)

The American beaver is the largest rodent in the U.S. Because of its strong front teeth, it can bring down trees by chewing into them at the base until they topple over. These teeth grow continuously throughout the beaver's life.

With the branches of the trees they knock over, beavers make dams, which they pack with mud so that no water can get through. A dam turns a small stream into a very large pond, creating an environment for all sorts of other animals to live in. The beavers themselves live in a "lodge" in the pond, which they make from sticks, branches, and mud.

SIZE: 2–3 ft. long

DIET: All parts of woody plants and trees, and aquatic plants such as water lilies

FOUND IN: Large freshwater wetlands that the beavers themselves create

NORTHERN FLICKER
(Colaptes auratus)

The northern flicker is a type of woodpecker. Yet unlike most woodpeckers, northern flickers do a lot of their feeding on the ground. They mainly eat ants, which they catch with their long tongue. This is covered in sticky saliva.

Some people call northern flickers "yellowhammers." This is partly because they have bright yellow feathers under their wings and tails, and partly because they drill (or "hammer") their beaks against trees. In the western U.S., however, these birds have red feathers under their wings and tails, rather than yellow.

SIZE: 1 ft. long; 20 in. wingspan

DIET: Mainly ants and beetles; also seeds and fruits

FOUND IN: Woodlands, yards, and parks

GREEN ANOLE
(Anolis carolinensis)

The green anole is normally lime green, but can change color to a brownish green or dark brown. Unlike chameleons, they don't change color to blend into their background, but rather in response to the temperature, their health, or the mood that they are in.

You can tell the male and a female green anole apart from the male's brightly colored throat. This can be pink, orange, or red. Females, in contrast, have a white throat. Males sometimes extend their colorful throats to show aggression to other nearby males, as well as to attract females.

SIZE: 5–9 in. long

YOUNG: The female lays one egg (in leaf litter) every two weeks throughout summer

FOUND IN: Almost anywhere, from forests and swamps to backyards and parks

EASTERN LUBBER GRASSHOPPER
(Romalea microptera)

The eastern lubber grasshopper is the largest grasshopper in North America, and is toxic to predators. Their bright color acts as a warning, as does the foul-smelling liquid they spray if picked up. This liquid isn't harmful to people, but the smell might make you wish you hadn't picked it up!

These grasshoppers eat many kinds of plants, and are often considered pests in people's gardens. They particularly like to eat the leaves of vegetables, including peas, lettuce, beans, tomatoes, and peppers.

SIZE: 2–3 in. long

EGGS: The female lays 100–250 eggs, 0.5 in. deep in the ground

FOUND IN: Swamps, weedy fields, and pine woods

Alaska

Alaska is the largest of the fifty states. It is more than two-and-a-half times larger than Texas, the second-largest state. Much of Alaska is wild and remote, untouched by humans. It is home to a great diversity of animals and plants, many of which are not found in any other state.

FIREWEED
(Epilobium angustifolium)

Fireweed flowers start blooming at the bottom of the stalk and make their way to the top of the plant. People say that you can track how much of summer is left based on how high the flowers are on the plant.

Fireweed is eaten by many different animals, including bears, deer, moose, caribou, and hares. A lot of bees, insects, and birds feed on fireweed nectar. Some people also eat young fireweed shoots like you would eat asparagus. You can also make tea from the dried leaves, and use the flower nectar in jellies, honey, and syrup.

HEIGHT: 2.5–5 ft.

SEASON: Blooms July–September

FOUND IN: Almost anywhere—open areas, roadsides, mountains, and in forests

SITKA SPRUCE
(Picea sitchensis)

Sitka spruce is the state tree of Alaska. It is also the tallest tree in the state. Sitka spruce trees tend to be very long-lived, with some alive today that are more than 1,000 years old! That means that some were more than 500 years old when the first Europeans set foot on what is now the United States of America.

Various animals eat Sitka spruce twigs and branches, including deer, elk, porcupines, and bears. A lot of small mammals (such as mice, voles, squirrels, and chipmunks) and many bird species eat the seeds from their cones.

HEIGHT: Can grow over 200 ft. tall (and can be more than 10 ft. across at the base)

SEASON: Has needles year-round

FOUND IN: Coastal areas, primarily

SALMONBERRY
(Rubus spectabilis)

Salmonberry is a short woody shrub that is common throughout much of the southern half of Alaska. Salmonberry shrubs grow in dense clusters and produce a lot of berries, which look very similar to raspberries. Ripe salmonberries can be red, orange, or yellow.

Salmonberry fruits were, and still are, very important to indigenous peoples in Alaska. They also are eaten by a wide variety of wildlife, including many different types of mammals (big and small) and birds. Many people enjoy eating salmonberries raw, as well as using them to make pies, pancakes, jellies, and syrups.

HEIGHT: 3–5 ft.

SEASON: Fruits ripen in mid- to late summer

FOUND IN: A wide variety of settings, including in meadows, mountain slopes, and in forests

ARCTIC WILLOW
(Salix arctica)

Most willow species grow as trees or tall shrubs. Arctic willow is quite different. It grows low along the ground as a creeping mat.

Arctic willow is an important food source for animals such as muskoxen, caribou, lemmings, Arctic hares, and ptarmigan (a type of ground-nesting bird). Indigenous communities have long used Arctic willow as a medicine to help to stop bleeding and for relieving toothaches and upset stomachs. They would also chew on the leaves (like you do with gum), or even eat them, since they are sweet and full of vitamin C.

HEIGHT: Up to 10 in.

SEASON: Flowers emerge at the same time as the leaves

FOUND IN: Areas of full sunlight

Alaska

SEA OTTER
(Enhydra lutris)

Sea otters spend almost their entire life in the water. The only exception is when they occasionally climb out onto the shore or a rock for a short rest. They even sleep while floating on the water. Often, they will sleep holding hands with another sea otter, so that they don't drift apart.

Sea otters dive underwater to catch their food. They can hold their breath for more than five minutes, and can dive as deep as 250 feet. They then use rocks to crack open the shells of their food. While diving, they sometimes store the rock in their armpit.

SIZE: Up to 5 ft. long

FOUND IN: Shallow, coastal ocean waters

DIET: Mainly shellfish such as sea urchins, mussels, clams, and crabs; also fish

MUSKOX
(Ovibos moschatus)

Muskoxen (the word for more than one muskox) live in herds, which helps protect them from grizzly bears and wolves. They spend much of their time feeding in wide-open tundra grasslands, eating many different types of plants.

Muskoxen have a super dense, long hairy coat over their entire body. This keeps them warm during the incredibly cold Alaskan winters. The fibers of the undercoat are very valuable to humans for yarn. Yarn from muskoxen is more than five times warmer than sheep's wool and is one of the softest fibers in the world.

SIZE: 4–5 ft. tall; 6–8 ft. long

FOUND IN: Northern Alaska in tundra, grasslands, and meadows

DIET: Grasses and small woody plants; roots, moss, and lichens in winter

BALD EAGLE
(Haliaeetus leucocephalus)

Bald eagles are not in fact bald. They were named more than 250 years ago, when the word "bald" meant "white-headed." Their head and tail feathers are brown until they are two years old, when they start to change color to white.

Adult bald eagles stay with the same mate for life. Together they build massive nests, which often are 4–5 feet wide and 3–4 feet tall. Their nests are made mainly of sticks and branches, and can weigh over 2,000 pounds. A pair will raise two to three young each year, which will go off to live on their own after being raised by their parents for two to three months.

SIZE: Up to 3 ft. long; 7 ft. wingspan

FOUND IN: Forests next to the ocean, rivers, and lakes

DIET: Mainly fish; also small mammals, ducks, and dead animals

WOOD FROG
(Lithobates sylvaticus)

The wood frog is the only amphibian that lives north of the Arctic Circle in Alaska. It survives the incredibly cold winters there because it makes its own anti-freeze. Almost half of its body freezes for up to eight months at a time. During this time, its heart stops beating and it stops breathing.

Each spring, after they thaw out, male wood frogs hop down to their breeding ponds, where they float on the surface and call out to attract females. Their calls sound just like ducks quacking.

SIZE: 2–2.5 in. long

EGGS: The female lays a roundish mass that contains as many as 3,000 eggs

FOUND IN: Forests, for most of their life; breeding happens in small freshwater wetlands that dry up in the summer

ARIZONA

Arizona has a very diverse mix of landscapes throughout the state. Southern Arizona is mostly desert. The elevation continually increases as you go north, and in central Arizona, you enter high, forested mountains. Northern Arizona is very dry and flat, except for the Grand Canyon. Because of these differences, Arizona has a great diversity of plant and animal species.

BLUE PALO VERDE
(Parkinsonia florida)

The blue palo verde is the state tree of Arizona. "Palo verde" means "green pole" in Spanish, and refers to the blue-green trunk and branches of the tree. Blue palo verde trees are important to the saguaro cacti that grow underneath, offering them shade and protection.

Many rodents and birds eat the beans of blue palo verde trees. Larger animals, such as mule deer, bighorn sheep, and burros, feed on their leaves and twigs. Many indigenous communities cook the beans whole, or grind them into flour. They also use the wood from these trees to carve wooden utensils, such as soup ladles.

HEIGHT: 30–40 ft.

FOUND IN: Mainly in the desert in washes

SEASON: Blooms in late spring

VELVET MESQUITE
(Neltuma velutina)

The velvet mesquite tree is able to survive in extremely dry areas. This is mainly because its main root, called a "taproot," can extend more than 100 feet below the ground. This allows it to access very deep groundwater.

The velvet mesquite tree is widely used by people. Charcoal made from its bark gives a delicious flavor to grilled food. Many people say that the honey from bees that pollinate velvet mesquite trees is some of the best in the world. Its bark is also popular for making baskets, and many people who live in dry areas plant the tree in their yard for shade.

HEIGHT: 20–50 ft.

FOUND IN: Desert grasslands near washes

SEASON: Flowers bloom in the spring

SAGUARO
(Carnegiea gigantea)

Saguaro is pronounced "sa-wah-ro." Swap the "gu" in the middle of its name with "w" to say it correctly. The saguaro is the largest cactus in the U.S., and its flower is the state flower of Arizona. Saguaros only exist in the Sonoran Desert and are very slow growing. It often takes them between 20–50 years to grow to 3 feet tall. They can live for 150–200 years.

Some saguaros have "arms" and some don't. Those that don't are called "spears." Saguaros have very sharp spines all over them, which can be up to 3 inches long. The main purpose of the spines is to keep animals from eating the cactus, but they also help the saguaro regulate its temperature.

Many animals rely on saguaros. Woodpeckers drill nest cavities in them, which are often used in future years by other bird species. Birds, bats, coyotes, jackrabbits, tortoises, and many other animals eat saguaro fruits. Animals such as bighorn sheep and mule deer will sometimes eat its flesh.

HEIGHT: 40–60 ft.

FOUND IN: The Sonoran Desert

SEASON: Flowers bloom in spring, followed by red fruits in the summer

ARIZONA

BLACK-TAILED JACKRABBIT
(Lepus californicus)

The black-tailed jackrabbit lives in very hot areas. To try to stay cool, it often spends the hottest part of the day in the shade, usually under a shrub or in tall grass. Its very large ears also help it cool off. When the jackrabbit is hot, its body sends more blood to the ears, which release the heat, cooling down its entire body.

Black-tailed jackrabbits tend to live together in groups. This is so that they can look out for predators together. These rabbits eat a lot of vegetation—scientists estimate that in one day, fifteen individuals can consume the same amount as a large cow!

SIZE: About 2 ft. long; ears 4–6 in. long

FOUND IN: Open, dry areas such as meadows, prairies, and desert scrublands

DIET: Grasses and a variety of other green vegetation (particularly alfalfa); also woody stems in winter

CACTUS WREN
(Campylorhynchus brunneicapillus)

The cactus wren is named because it builds its nest on top of cacti, most often the cholla cactus. Sometimes these birds will nest inside holes in large cacti, such as saguaro. The nest is the size and shape of a football, and has an opening in one end. The wrens line the inside of this nest with feathers and, unlike most other birds, live in it year-round.

The cactus wren finds most of its food on the ground, flipping over small rocks and leaves with its bill. Because it is so dry where it lives, it gets most of its water from food.

SIZE: 7–8 in. long; 11 in. wingspan

FOUND IN: Deserts and scrublands

DIET: Mainly insects and sometimes small lizards; also berries, fruits, and seeds

GILA MONSTER
(Heloderma suspectum)

The gila monster is the largest lizard in North America, and the only venomous lizard in the U.S. The gila monster uses its venom to protect itself from predators. Scientists have recently discovered a chemical in this venom that helps treat diabetes in humans. This chemical is now manufactured for use in medications.

Gila monsters spend almost all their time hidden in burrows, caves, and other cool, safe spots. They commonly eat ten or fewer meals in a year. Because they store large amounts of fat in their thick tails, this is more than enough to sustain them.

SIZE: 18–22 in. long

DIET: Small mammals, lizards, frogs, birds, and birds' eggs

FOUND IN: Desert grasslands, scrublands, and canyons

GIANT DESERT HAIRY SCORPION
(Hadrurus arizonensis)

The giant desert hairy scorpion is the largest scorpion in North America. In the daytime, it lives in an underground burrow as deep as 8 feet. These scorpions are active aboveground at night, mainly to hunt. They eat other scorpions, insects, spiders, and small lizards and snakes, using their pincers to crush most of their prey. They only use their venom for larger prey, though this is fairly weak.

Female giant desert hairy scorpions give birth to twenty-five to thirty young. These will stay on their mother's back for their first one to three weeks of life, until their shells harden.

SIZE: Up to 7 in. long

FOUND IN: Deserts

YOUNG: The female gives birth to 25–35 live young (after a 6–12 month gestation period!)

Arkansas

Arkansas divides into three ecoregions of similar size. Much of northwestern Arkansas is forested mountains and hills. Eastern Arkansas is part of the Mississippi River floodplain, with a mix of forests, wetlands, and farms, and southern Arkansas is quite flat and mostly forested. Distinct plant and animal communities live in these different ecoregions.

LOBLOLLY PINE
(Pinus taeda)

Loblolly pine is the state tree of Arkansas. The word "loblolly" is a slang word for a swampy area, which is where the tree is often found. It is the second-most common tree species in the U.S., behind only the red maple.

The loblolly pine is one of the largest pine tree species in the southern U.S. It grows quickly, usually at a rate of 2 feet per year. Because of this, and because its wood is of high quality, loblolly pine trees are used widely for lumber.

HEIGHT: Up to 125 ft.

SEASON: Has needles year-round

FOUND IN: Areas of moist to wet soils with full sun exposure

AMERICAN BEAUTYBERRY
(Callicarpa americana)

The American beautyberry is best known for its glossy purple berries, which appear in the fall and grow in many large clusters along the branches. The berries are a very important food source for many bird species, and are also eaten by various mammals. These include armadillos, raccoons, foxes, and opossums.

Indigenous communities have historically made teas from plant parts, and used these to treat many conditions. These include stomach aches, dizziness, fever, and arthritis pain. Farmers used to crush the leaves and use them to repel mosquitoes.

HEIGHT: 4–8 ft.

SEASON: Flowers bloom in the summer; fruits appear in fall and stay on into the winter

FOUND IN: Open meadows and thickets; also along edges of streams, ditches, and ponds

POSSUMHAW
(Ilex decidua)

Possumhaw is a type of holly. Most holly species are evergreen, which means they keep their leaves all year round, but possumhaw drops its leaves in the winter. This has led to it often being called "deciduous holly." "Deciduous" is a term used to describe a shrub or tree that drops its leaves each year.

Possumhaw is well known for the bright-red berries that the female plants produce. These will remain on the plant through winter, if they are not eaten by wildlife. The "possum" part of its name comes from the fact that opossums like to eat the berries, as do other wildlife. People will often plant possumhaw in yards as an ornamental plant, since its bright-red fruits are so pretty in the fall and winter.

HEIGHT: Most commonly 10–20 ft.

SEASON: Flowers bloom early spring; fruits appear in summer, redden in fall, and remain well into winter

FOUND IN: A range of settings; most frequently in bottomland areas

FIRE PINK
(Silene virginica)

Fire pink flowers are mostly pollinated by hummingbirds, which are attracted to this specific type of flower: red or purple with a tubular shape.

A common nickname for fire pink is "scarlet catchfly." This refers to the red color of the flowers, and the sticky, insect-catching hairs on the leaves under the flower. These hairs are very good at stopping ants from reaching the flowers to steal their nectar.

HEIGHT: 1–2 ft.

SEASON: Blooms in late spring through summer

FOUND IN: Woodlands, rocky slopes, and meadows

Arkansas

EASTERN GRAY SQUIRREL
(Sciurus carolinensis)

Gray squirrels live in many places, including forests, parks, and yards. They are found wherever there are trees that produce nuts, and are even common in cities. These squirrels will bury a large number of nuts, some of which they come back to find and eat later. A single squirrel can hide about 10,000 nuts in a year. Because they don't retrieve all the nuts they bury, many of these nuts grow into trees.

Most eastern gray squirrels are, as the name suggests, gray, but some are black, and very rarely they can be white. They make their homes high up in trees, either inside tree cavities or in nests that they build from leaves and twigs.

SIZE: 15–20 in. long

DIET: Mainly nuts such as acorns, beech nuts, and hickory nuts

FOUND IN: Deciduous forests and suburban and urban areas that have nut-producing trees

NORTHERN MOCKINGBIRD
(Mimus polyglottos)

Northern mockingbirds are thus named because they can mimic (or "mock") other birds' songs. They have been observed imitating the songs of hundreds of other bird species. Some have also been heard imitating car alarms and police sirens, as well as dogs barking, frog calls, and other sounds. Scientists believe that the female selects her mate based on his ability to imitate the songs of other birds.

Northern mockingbirds have very noticeable white wing patches, which scientists think they flash to startle insects, which they then eat. They also use these wing patches in displays to defend their territory.

SIZE: 10 in. long; 14 in. wingspan

DIET: Mainly insects during the summer; berries, fruits, and seeds the rest of the year

FOUND IN: Open areas that have some shrubs and/or thickets, such as meadows, yards, and parks

THREE-TOED BOX TURTLE
(Terrapene carolina triunguis)

The three-toed box turtle usually, but not always, has three toes on each of its hind feet, whereas most other box turtle species have four. The name "box turtle" comes from the hinges on its bottom shell, which lets it close up completely, like a box, to protect itself from predators.

Three-toed box turtles live almost their entire life on land, like tortoises. Sometimes, during really hot times of the year, they will seek out water or mud to cool off in.

SIZE: 4–6 in. long

EGGS: The female lays 1–7 eggs underground in a nest she digs

FOUND IN: Forests that have shallow water sources nearby

PIPEVINE SWALLOWTAIL
(Battus philenor)

The pipevine swallowtail butterfly gets its name from the vine "Dutchman's pipe," which its caterpillars feed on. People also call this species the "blue swallowtail" because of its bright blue color. This bright coloration is a warning to predators that the butterfly is poisonous. The caterpillars absorb toxins from the leaves they eat, which make them, and the butterflies they turn into, poisonous.

Other non-poisonous butterflies look similar to pipevine swallowtail butterflies. This is thought to be a trick to warn off predators from eating them.

SIZE: 1–1.5 in. long; 3–5 in. wingspan

EGGS: The female lays a group of eggs (often less than 20) on the underside of Dutchman's pipe leaves

FOUND IN: Open areas ranging from open woodlands to meadows

CALIFORNIA

California is the third-largest state in the United States, behind only Alaska and Texas in size. Its size, and its many different landscape types, make this state home to many different animals and plants. California has ocean, mountains, valleys, deserts, rivers, lakes, and more.

COAST REDWOOD
(Sequoia sempervirens)

The coast redwood tree is the state tree of California and the tallest type of tree in the world. These trees can also live for more than 2,000 years! They tend to exist in fire-prone areas, but they often survive fires thanks to their thick bark, which can be as thick as 12 inches (1 foot).

Often, branches high up in redwood trees create their own ecosystem. Debris such as smaller branches, sticks, and needles pile up on these branches, turning them into large mats, sometimes hundreds of feet above the ground. Many plants grow on these, including mosses, ferns, shrubs, and even small trees. Many different types of animals, including birds, bats, and small mammals form part of these ecosystems. A particular kind of salamander, called the "wandering salamander," is often found in these canopy mat areas, sometimes spending their entire lives there without ever touching the ground!

HEIGHT: Up to 350 ft.

SEASON: Has needles year-round

FOUND IN: Foggy and moist coastal areas from central California to southern Oregon

GIANT SEQUOIA
(Sequoiadendron giganteum)

Giant sequoia trees can live up to about 3,000 years old! They are the heaviest trees in the world, weighing about 640 tons. That's as heavy as about a hundred adult African elephants!

Like redwood trees, giant sequoias are able to survive most fires. This is mainly because of their very thick bark. This bark can be as thick as 18 inches (1.5 feet). Giant sequoias rely on fire to reproduce. Their seeds are inside their cones, which hang in the trees for as long as twenty years and only emerge when the cones fully dry out. This drying often happens one to two weeks after a fire.

HEIGHT: Up to 300 ft.

FOUND IN: Western slopes of the Sierra Nevada mountains

SEASON: Has needles year-round

CALIFORNIA POPPY
(Eschscholzia californica)

The California poppy is the state flower of California. It is sometimes called the "golden poppy" due to its bright gold flowers. Sometimes, following heavy rainstorms, something called a "super bloom" occurs, when a huge number California poppies sprout. Some of these super blooms are so magnificent that tens of thousands of people will come to view them.

The California poppy is considered a symbol of California. It is often painted on highway signs welcoming people to the state. April 6, a California state holiday, is called "California Poppy Day" in celebration of the beautiful flower.

HEIGHT: 5–12 in.

FOUND IN: Sunny meadows

SEASON: Blooms in late spring and summer

CALIFORNIA

STELLER SEA LION
(*Eumetopias jubatus*)

The number of Steller sea lions in the wild today is much lower it used to be, though that number is increasing thanks to efforts to protect the species. They are currently classified as endangered. They are very social creatures, and are often seen in large groups together. Males can live up to about twenty years old, and females about thirty.

Steller sea lions live in coastal areas and eat mainly fish—more than a hundred different species of them. The sea lions can dive as deep as 1,000 feet or more to catch fish.

SIZE: Up to 9 ft. long (females); up to 11 ft. long (males)

FOUND IN: Coastal waters, often with rocky shorelines and/or small exposed rocky islands

DIET: A wide variety of fish

ACORN WOODPECKER
(*Melanerpes formicivorus*)

Scientists named the acorn woodpecker for its habit of storing acorns and other nuts in trees as a winter food store. These woodpeckers drill holes into the trees with their bills, storing a nut in each one. They can sometimes store more than 10,000 nuts in a single tree! These trees are referred to as their "granaries."

Acorn woodpeckers live together in family groups, which may contain ten or more individuals. They work together to collect, store, and guard their food, and to raise their young.

SIZE: 8–9 in. long; 14–17 in. wingspan

FOUND IN: Oak and pine-oak forests and woodlands

DIET: Mainly acorns and a wide variety of insects (especially ants)

SIDEWINDER
(Crotalus cerastes)

The sidewinder is a rattlesnake that lives in the Mojave Desert of the U.S. as well as northern Mexico. It has this name because it moves sideways rather than forward like most snakes do. This movement in an S-shape minimizes the amount the snake's body touches the hot desert sand. Because it lives in such hot areas, it is active mainly at night, and inactive during mid-summer when it is hottest.

Sidewinders give birth to young rather than laying eggs—typically between four and twelve. These young live entirely on their own immediately after being born.

SIZE: 1–2.5 ft. long

FOUND IN: Sandy desert areas

DIET: Rodents and lizards

PACIFIC BANANA SLUG
(Ariolimax columbianus)

The Pacific banana slug is the second-longest land slug in the world. The ash-black slug of the United Kingdom is the longest, though it's only about an inch longer. Scientists named it the Pacific banana slug because it is banana-shaped, yellow or brown, and sometimes even has spots like a ripe banana. This coloration and pattern helps the slug to camouflage among decaying leaves and needles on the forest floor.

The Pacific banana slug is covered in a very sticky liquid, which helps protect it from many predators. This liquid can numb the tongue and throat of predators such as snakes, salamanders, and birds, causing them to spit out the slug. It also can glue the predator's mouth closed for a short time.

SIZE: Up to 10 in. long

FOUND IN: Moist, dense forests

EGGS: Lays as many as 75 eggs in leaves or in logs

Colorado

Colorado can look very different depending on where you are in the state. Most of the eastern part of the state is prairies, whereas the Rocky Mountains make up much of central Colorado, and western Colorado is quite dry, mainly with grasses and sparse low shrubs. These different parts of Colorado are home to different plant and animal species.

COLORADO BLUE SPRUCE
(Picea pungens)

The Colorado blue spruce is the state tree of Colorado, and gets its name from its blue-green needles. People in indigenous communities have used the needle's liquid to treat colds and stomach aches. They also apply it to the skin to reduce arthritis pain.

Colorado blue spruce trees grow very slowly, and can live more than 600 years. They can tolerate extreme cold, even as cold as 40 degrees below freezing. They are often planted as an ornamental tree in yards, thanks to their attractive needles and their ability to survive very cold temperatures.

HEIGHT: Up to 75 ft.

FOUND IN: High elevations in the Rocky Mountains

SEASON: Has needles year-round

COLORADO COLUMBINE
(Aquilegia coerulea)

The Colorado columbine is the state flower of Colorado. It is one of the most photographed wildflowers because of how beautiful it is. The name "columbine" comes from the Latin word for "dove" since, when you look at the flower from behind as it is facing down, it looks like doves drinking from a fountain.

Colorado columbine flowers are most often pollinated by bumblebees and hawkmoths. Hawkmoths are large moths with a 3–4 inch wingspan. Hawkmoths are sometimes called "hummingbird moths," as they hover like hummingbirds when feeding from flowers.

HEIGHT: 1–2.5 ft.

FOUND IN: Mid- to high-elevation areas in open forests, meadows, and rocky slopes

SEASON: Blooms late spring through summer

RUBBER RABBITBRUSH
(Ericameria nauseosa)

Rubber rabbitbrush is a shrub that gets the "rubber" part of its name from its sap, which contains a type of rubber that is used in various products. Indigenous communities use rubber rabbitbrush as chewing gum. They also make yellow dye, medicinal tea, and cough syrup from it.

Some animals, like mule deer, pronghorn, and jackrabbits, feed on rubber rabbitbrush, especially in the fall and winter. Small mammals and many birds also use it to hide from predators, as well as a source of shade on hot, sunny days.

HEIGHT: 6–25 ft.

SEASON: Blooms late summer and fall

FOUND IN: Sunny, dry, and disturbed areas such as roadsides and rangelands

SHOWY MILKWEED
(Asclepias speciosa)

This flower gets the "milk" in its name from the milky-colored sap contained in the plant and its leaves. This sap is poisonous to most animals, which keeps them from eating it.

One exception is the monarch butterfly, which lays its eggs on milkweed, and the caterpillars eat it leaves after they've hatched. Rather than harming the caterpillars, it makes them poisonous, including when they turn into butterflies. The adult monarch butterfly has a bright orange color, which warns to birds and other predators of the poison.

HEIGHT: 4–6 ft.

SEASON: Flowers bloom in summer

FOUND IN: Sunny and dry areas such as fields and roadsides

Colorado

AMERICAN PIKA
(Ochotona princeps)

The American pika lives in rocky areas high up in mountains. Pikas live in colonies and make warning calls to other pikas when a predator is nearby, but within the colony, each pika lives alone in its own den. The only exception is when a mother pika shares her den with her babies for their first month of life.

Pikas don't hibernate, though they spend much of the winter inside their dens. During the summer, they collect a lot of extra food, mainly grasses and wildflowers, which they store in their dens for the winter after first drying it out so that it doesn't get moldy.

SIZE: 6–8 in. long

DIET: A variety of grasses, sedges, and herbaceous plants

FOUND IN: High-elevation, rocky areas (typically above the treeline)

RED-TAILED HAWK
(Buteo jamaicensis)

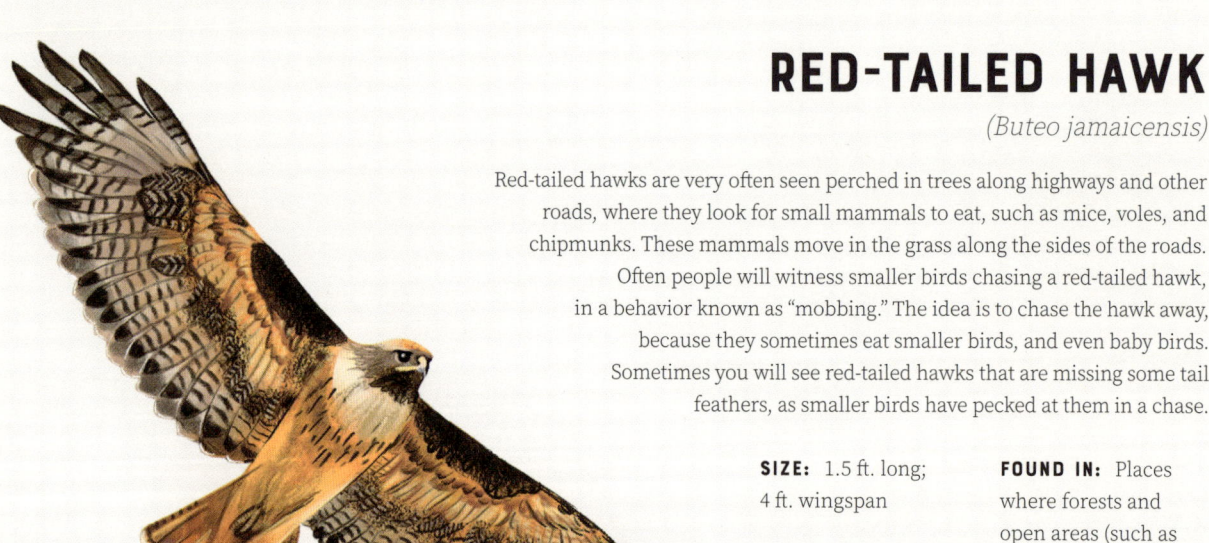

Red-tailed hawks are very often seen perched in trees along highways and other roads, where they look for small mammals to eat, such as mice, voles, and chipmunks. These mammals move in the grass along the sides of the roads. Often people will witness smaller birds chasing a red-tailed hawk, in a behavior known as "mobbing." The idea is to chase the hawk away, because they sometimes eat smaller birds, and even baby birds. Sometimes you will see red-tailed hawks that are missing some tail feathers, as smaller birds have pecked at them in a chase.

SIZE: 1.5 ft. long; 4 ft. wingspan

DIET: Mainly small mammals (such as mice and squirrels), birds, and snakes

FOUND IN: Places where forests and open areas (such as fields and meadows) meet

PRAIRIE RATTLESNAKE
(Crotalus viridis)

As its name suggests, the prairie rattlesnake lives in open areas like prairies. It is the most widespread rattlesnake species in the United States, found throughout much of the area known as the Great Plains. Prairie rattlesnakes are found, in particular, through much of Montana and North Dakota, but extend southward into Arizona, New Mexico, and Texas.

Like other rattlesnakes, prairie rattlesnakes track their warm prey with heat-sensing pits, located between their eyes and nostrils. Before eating it, they kill this prey with venom that they inject with their fangs.

SIZE: 3–5 ft. long

DIET: Mainly small mammals and birds; the young will often eat amphibians and reptiles

FOUND IN: Mostly in prairies and grasslands; also shrublands, forests, and nearby rivers

CONVERGENT LADY BEETLE
(Hippodamia convergens)

The convergent lady beetle is one of about eighty kinds of lady beetle—often called "lady bugs"—found in Colorado. The convergent lady beetle is one of the most numerous beetles in all the U.S., and can be found in almost all states, including Hawaii and Alaska.

Like many lady beetles, the convergent lady beetle is very important for agriculture, as it eats small bugs called aphids that feed on many crops, causing them a lot of damage. By controlling aphid populations, lady beetles help the crops grow better.

SIZE: Up to 0.25 in. long

EGGS: The female will lay 200–1,000 eggs in small clusters (typically less than 30 eggs in one cluster) on plants with aphids; the aphids will be food for the young

FOUND IN: A wide range of areas including gardens, yards, parks, meadows, and even open forests

CONNECTICUT

Connecticut's landscape is diverse. It has coastal areas, deciduous and coniferous forests, rivers, flatlands, hills, and more. It also has a good mix of rural, suburban, and urban areas. As a result, many different plants and animals call Connecticut home.

WHITE OAK
(Quercus alba)

The white oak is the state tree of Connecticut. These grow quite slowly, and can live for up to 500 years, or even a little more. White oak trees have very strong wood and are well known for their acorns. Some years, a single white oak can produce thousands of acorns! Acorns are a very important food source for many animals, including squirrels, chipmunks, deer, blue jays, turkeys, ducks, and more.

HEIGHT: 80–100 ft.

SEASON: Drops acorns from late summer through fall; drops leaves for winter

FOUND IN: A wide range of settings, preferably areas with a lot of sunlight

MOUNTAIN LAUREL
(Kalmia latifolia)

The mountain laurel grows as a shrub in Connecticut, but can also grow as a tree farther south. Often, many grow together in dense thickets, which animals use for shelter. Black bears, for example, have been found to den over the winter in dense mountain laurel thickets.

Mountain laurels are "evergreen," keeping their leaves all year long. In spring, they are covered in beautiful white flowers speckled with pink. The flower of the mountain laurel is the state flower of Connecticut.

HEIGHT: 6–10 ft. (shrub); up to 40 ft. (tree)

SEASON: Flowers in the spring; keeps leaves year-round

FOUND IN: Acidic soils on rocky slopes and mountainous forested settings

NORTHERN SPICEBUSH
(Lindera benzoin)

Northern spicebush shrubs are one of the first plants to flower each spring. Their flowers are bright yellow and appear even before their leaves have begun to emerge. The nectar from these flowers is a vital early season food for many bees and flies.

Northern spicebush's name comes from its spicy, citrusy scent, which you can smell if you rub the leaves between your fingers. Some people make a citrus-like tea with the leaves. You can also dry out and grind the fruits to make a spice.

HEIGHT: 6–12 ft.

SEASON: Flowers in early spring; drops leaves for the winter

FOUND IN: The understory of woodlands with rich soil

AMERICAN POKEWEED
(Phytolacca americana)

American pokeweed produces abundant berries when it fruits in the fall. These berries are very poisonous to humans—even eating a single one could cause serious harm! Various birds can eat them, however, without being poisoned. In fact, they are an important food source for northern mockingbirds, northern cardinals, mourning doves, and others. Even some mammals such as raccoons, opossums, and foxes can eat the berries. The berries are sometimes used to make natural dyes for wool and yarns, which come out in a variety of shades of pink and purple.

HEIGHT: 4–10 ft.

FOUND IN: Open or edge areas with moist soils

SEASON: Flowers from summer into fall; fruits from late summer into fall

CONNECTICUT

AMERICAN RED SQUIRREL
(Tamiasciurus hudsonicus)

American red squirrels are often found on, or near, conifer trees. This is because they mainly eat seeds from inside the cones of these trees. They spend a lot of time in the summer and fall collecting cones for the winter, which they store in a large pile of cone scales and other debris called a "midden." This keeps the cones in the midden, stored in their hundreds and sometimes thousands, from drying out and releasing their seeds. Each red squirrel will fiercely defend their midden from other animals, including other red squirrels.

SIZE: 10–14 in. long; 4–5 in. tail

DIET: Nuts, seeds, and fruits

FOUND IN: Coniferous forests and deciduous forests with conifer trees

SNAPPING TURTLE
(Chelydra serpentina)

The snapping turtle is the second-largest freshwater turtle in the U.S. (the alligator snapping turtle is the largest). Some have lived to be a hundred years old! They live most of their lives in the water, which they only leave to travel between two wetlands or, in the case of the female, to lay eggs on land.

Snapping turtles are named for their very powerful jaws, which they use to snap at and catch food with. They are often mistakenly believed to be dangerous to people, but as long as you are not bothering them, they won't bother you.

SIZE: 1–1.5 ft.

EGGS: The female lays 25–40 eggs underground

FOUND IN: Almost any type of freshwater wetland

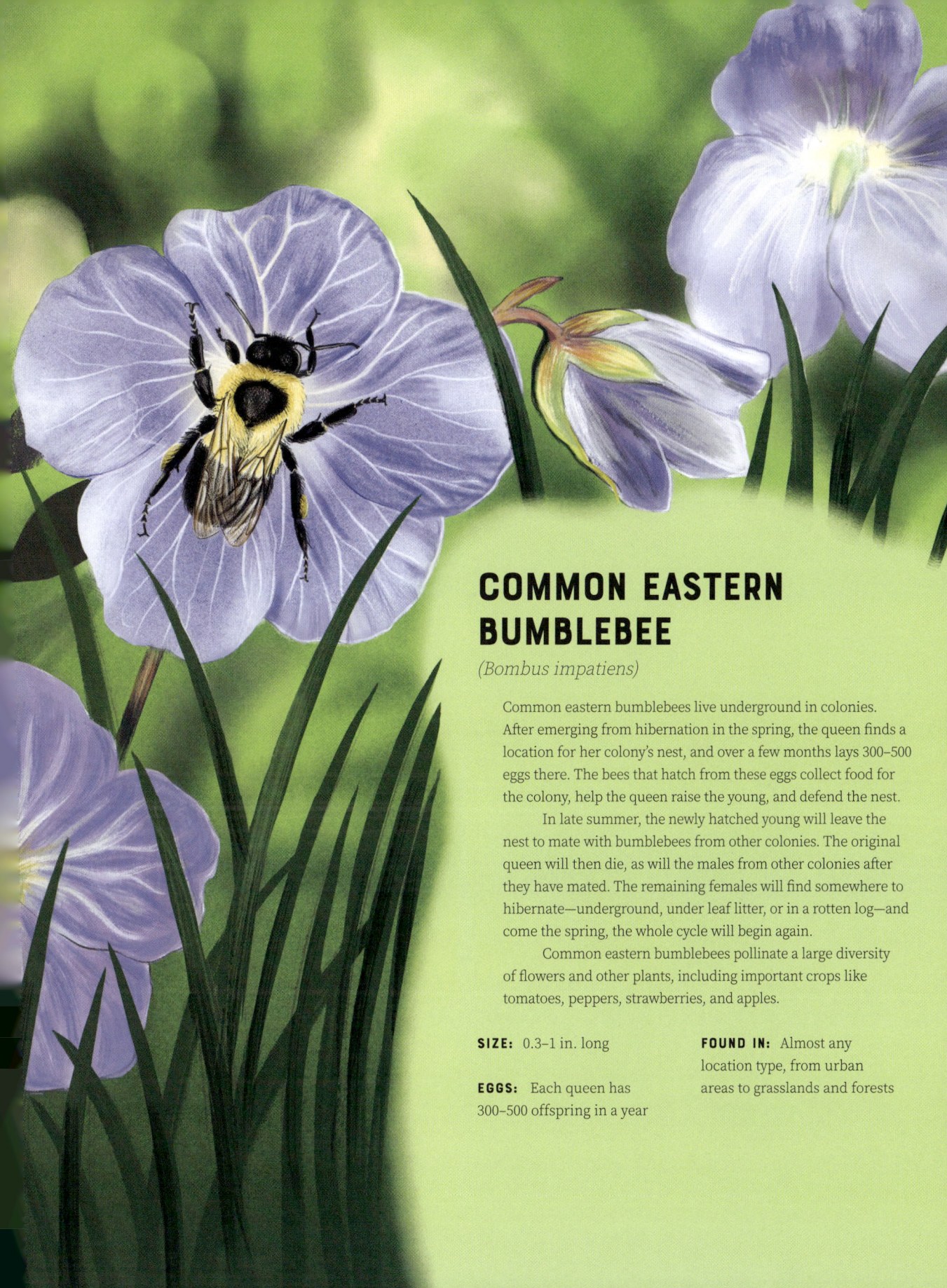

COMMON EASTERN BUMBLEBEE
(Bombus impatiens)

Common eastern bumblebees live underground in colonies. After emerging from hibernation in the spring, the queen finds a location for her colony's nest, and over a few months lays 300–500 eggs there. The bees that hatch from these eggs collect food for the colony, help the queen raise the young, and defend the nest.

In late summer, the newly hatched young will leave the nest to mate with bumblebees from other colonies. The original queen will then die, as will the males from other colonies after they have mated. The remaining females will find somewhere to hibernate—underground, under leaf litter, or in a rotten log—and come the spring, the whole cycle will begin again.

Common eastern bumblebees pollinate a large diversity of flowers and other plants, including important crops like tomatoes, peppers, strawberries, and apples.

SIZE: 0.3–1 in. long

EGGS: Each queen has 300–500 offspring in a year

FOUND IN: Almost any location type, from urban areas to grasslands and forests

Delaware

Delaware is the second-smallest state in the U.S. by land area. Despite this, it is home to a huge range of animals and plants! This is partly due to its wonderfully diverse range of habitats. Delaware has saltwater coastal areas, inshore coastal areas (found along Delaware Bay), and a range of inland habitats, too.

AMERICAN SWEETGUM
(Liquidambar styraciflua)

The wood of the American sweetgum tree is very pretty—a bright reddish-brown color with interesting patterns, it is often used for furniture.

American sweetgum get its name from the resin (a liquid, like sap) inside of it. This resin smells very sweet and used to be made into chewing gum.

Sweetgums have unique-looking fruits, which are round and covered in spikes. These go by many different names, including "gumballs," "space bugs," and "spike balls."

HEIGHT: 60–100 ft. tall

FOUND IN: Areas with deep and moist soils

SEASON: Drops leaves for the winter; drops fruits from late fall through winter

AMERICAN HOLLY
(Ilex opaca)

The American holly is the state tree of Delaware. Many people associate it with Christmas, since holly branches are so often used in holiday decorations. You will likely recognize their shiny evergreen leaves and bright-red berries.

American holly trees provide a great source of winter fruit for a lot of different animals, including various types of birds and small mammals. Its abundant fruits attract some beautiful birds in the winter, such as cedar waxwings, bluebirds, and American robins.

HEIGHT: 15–30 ft. (shrub); up to 100 ft. (tree)

FOUND IN: A wide range of settings; often in the understory

SEASON: Flowers in spring; keeps leaves year-round

GREAT BLUE LOBELIA
(Lobelia siphilitica)

Great blue lobelia is also known as the "blue cardinal flower." Many people plant these in their wildflower gardens because, when they bloom, they are covered in lots of beautiful violet-blue flowers. These flowers attract many kinds of butterflies and bees, and are one of the best flowers to attract hummingbirds with.

Great blue lobelia is also popular because it is resistant to being eaten by rabbits and deer. This is because the plant is toxic to them, which is signaled by its bitter taste.

HEIGHT: 2–3 ft.

FOUND IN: Wet areas and along wetland edges

SEASON: Flowers from late summer to early fall

LOW PRICKLY PEAR
(Opuntia humifusa)

The low prickly pear is one of the only native cacti in the eastern U.S., and is the only cactus found in every one of the lower forty-eight states. Low prickly pear is named for its fruit, which is the size and shape of a small pear and has fine, prickly hairs. Both the "pads" (the main part of the plant) and the fruit are edible to humans. Some say it tastes like melon or kiwi, with a hint of bubblegum flavor.

HEIGHT: 1–1.5 ft.

FOUND IN: Dry, exposed, sandy areas

SEASON: Flowers any time from spring to summer; fruits from late summer to early fall

Delaware

TRICOLORED BAT
(Perimyotis subflavus)

The tricolored bat is one of the smallest bats in the U.S., about the weight of a quarter. The tricolored bat gets its name from the three colors on each of its hairs: yellow, black, and reddish brown.

Tricolored bat populations have dramatically declined since 2007, as have other bat species. This is because of infection by a fungus that causes them to be active in the winter when they should be hibernating. Sadly, this causes many of the bats to starve to death.

SIZE: 3 in. long; 8–10 in. wingspan

FOUND IN: Locations with a mix of trees and open areas

YOUNG: Usually 2 young in a litter per year

DOUBLE-CRESTED CORMORANT
(Nannopterum auritum)

Double-crested cormorants are fast swimmers, with webbed feet that help propel them as they're chasing fish underwater. They have a sharply downward-hooked tip to their upper bill, which helps them catch fish, as well as helping them climb rocks.

When they are not in the water, cormorants often stand with their wings spread on rocks and jetties. They do this to help dry their feathers.

SIZE: 2.5 ft. long; 4 ft. wingspan

FOUND IN: Shallow saltwater areas; also large lakes and reservoirs

DIET: Fish

EASTERN SPADEFOOT TOAD

(Scaphiopus holbrookii)

Eastern spadefoot toads have a spade-like growth on the bottom of each of their hind feet, which they use to burrow underground. These toads spend most of their lives entirely underground, only coming out at night to feed, or, rarely, to breed. When they do breed, they do so in wetlands, or sometimes even in puddles. Unlike almost all other frogs and toads, they don't breed every year.

SIZE: 2–2.5 in. long

EGGS: 1,000–2,500 eggs

FOUND IN: Sandy areas, underground; breeding takes place in quickly drying wetlands and puddles

EASTERN HARVESTMAN

(Leiobunum vittatum)

The eastern harvestman is often called a "daddy long-legs." Many people think they are spiders, but actually they aren't. There is also a popular myth that eastern harvestmen have fangs and are venomous. This is also untrue. Eastern harvestmen are active mainly at night, usually to hunt. Rather than making webs to catch food, like spiders do, they actively look for it themselves. Eastern harvestmen eat many different types of insects, which can be helpful to humans. If you see one in your garage or basement, don't be scared—they can't bite you!

SIZE: Body is 0.25–0.5 in. long, with much longer legs

EGGS: The female lays eggs in moss, rotting wood, or moist soil; these take 1–2 months to hatch

FOUND IN: Forests, stone walls, basements, and garages

FLORIDA

Florida is one of the more biodiverse states. The southernmost state in the continental U.S., it contains a range of ecosystems, habitats, and larger ecoregions. It also has a huge amount of coastline, along both the Atlantic Ocean and the Gulf of Mexico.

SABAL PALM
(Sabal palmetto)

The sabal palm is the state tree of Florida. Sabal palm trees have the characteristic palm tree structure, with crossed-hatched shaggy outer "bark" and a fan-shaped leaf structure on top. The bark segments are remnant leaf stalks, which will eventually fall off and expose the actual bark of the tree.

Sabal palm is very tolerant of salty winds, and can therefore often survive at the upper edges of beaches. It cannot, however, survive regular flooding by saltwater.

HEIGHT: 40–80 ft.

SEASON: Flowers in spring; keeps leaves year-round

FOUND IN: A wide range of settings from coastal dunes to pinelands to floodplain forests

ORANGE
(Citrus sinensis)

The orange tree is not native to the U.S., but was brought to Florida in the mid-1500s by Spanish colonizers, along with other citrus fruits such as lemons and limes.

Florida is now one of the biggest producers of oranges in the world, with many of its oranges turned into orange juice. The flower of the orange tree, known as an orange blossom, is the state flower of Florida. Orange blossoms are very fragrant and are used in many perfumes.

HEIGHT: 10–30 ft.

SEASON: Flowers in the spring; most fruits are harvested in fall/winter

FOUND IN: Grown in orchards/groves in the southern two-thirds of Florida

PICKERELWEED
(Pontederia cordata)

Pickerelweed flowers add a beautiful lavender color to many freshwater wetlands. They bloom for a long time, usually from early summer through much of the fall. Their flowers attract many insect pollinators, and many animals feed on other parts of the plant. These include ducks, geese, muskrats, and deer.

Pickerelweed is named after the chain pickerel, a common freshwater fish that often hides in the plant to ambush smaller fish.

HEIGHT: 3–4 ft.

SEASON: Flowers from summer to fall

FOUND IN: Wetland edges and in shallow portions of wetlands

SHINY BLUEBERRY
(Vaccinium myrsinites)

Shiny blueberry is a low and sprawling evergreen shrub. It has lots of flowers in the spring that attract many different pollinators. The flowers then become numerous blueberries that are eaten by many different types of mammals and birds. They include bears, raccoons, foxes, squirrels, jays, catbirds, bluebirds, and turkeys. Its seeds are mainly spread in the droppings of these animals.

Shiny blueberry grows into large colonies by extensive underground root systems. It is adapted to wildfires, and is one of the first plants to sprout after a wildfire moves through.

HEIGHT: 1–2 ft.

SEASON: Flowers in mid-spring; fruits from late spring to early summer; keeps leaves year-round

FOUND IN: Areas of dry, sandy, acidic soils with abundant sunlight

FLORIDA

WEST INDIAN MANATEE
(Trichechus manatus)

West Indian manatees are most often simply referred to as "manatees," or sometimes "sea cows," because they feed on aquatic plants. They spend their entire life in the water, and can hold their breath underwater for up to ten minutes!

Manatees live both in fresh water and salt water. They spend up to eight hours a day eating around 30 pounds of plants.

The West Indian manatee is listed as a "threatened" species under the U.S. Endangered Species Act. Though populations in Florida have been growing in the past two to three decades, hundreds still die every year from unnatural causes. Their main threats are accidental boat strikes, getting tangled in fishing gear, and reduced seagrass beds due to water pollution.

SIZE: 9–10 ft. long

FOUND IN: Shallow, slow-moving coastal waterways

YOUNG: Aquatic plants

FLORIDA PANTHER
(Puma concolor coryi)

The only wild mountain lion left in the eastern U.S. is the Florida panther. This is a critically endangered species, with only about 200 wild individuals alive today. Between the mid-1800s and 1950, they were almost hunted to extinction, with their population dropping as low as twenty to thirty individuals in the early 1970s.

Most of the wild Florida panthers alive today live in the southwestern tip of Florida. Their biggest threats are being hit by cars and habitat loss from urban development.

SIZE: 6–7 ft. long; males are larger than females

FOUND IN: Forests and swamplands of southern Florida

DIET: Mainly deer, feral hogs, raccoons, and armadillos

EASTERN INDIGO SNAKE
(Drymarchon couperi)

The indigo snake is the longest snake in the U.S. It gets its name from the purplish color it appears in sunlight. It is listed as a "threatened" species under the U.S. Endangered Species Act.

Indigo snakes spend most of their life underground in gopher tortoise burrows, often living there at the same time as the gopher tortoises themselves! These underground burrows provide a location that has steady temperatures throughout the year, and are also a safe place from predators.

SIZE: 6–8 ft. long; males are larger than females

FOUND IN: A range of habitats in Florida and southeastern Georgia

EGGS: The female lays 4–14 eggs in sandy soil and/or in gopher tortoise burrows

Georgia

Georgia is the second-largest state in the southeastern U.S., only slightly smaller than Florida. It contains a diverse range of ecosystems, thanks to varied elevation across the state. Much of the southern half of Georgia and its coastal regions are below 500 feet. As you move northward, elevation consistently increases, and by the time you reach the Appalachian Mountains in the north, you're 3,000 to 4,000 feet above sea level!

SOUTHERN LIVE OAK
(Quercus virginiana)

The southern live oak is the state tree of Georgia. An enormous tree, its "crown" (the top part) can often be 100 feet or more across. Southern live oaks differ from most oaks as they usually don't lose their leaves in winter, dropping them in early spring instead. Within a month or two, these leaves have already been replaced by fresh ones.

HEIGHT: 40–60 ft.

FOUND IN: Coastal plains, often in salty soils

SEASON: Flowers in spring; drops acorns in the fall; drops leaves in early spring

PEACH TREE
(Prunus persica)

The peach is the state fruit of Georgia—known as "the peach state"—and is often used as its symbol. Peach trees are originally from China, and were brought to Florida in the late 1500s by Spanish colonizers. They soon became popular and were planted throughout the eastern U.S.

As well as being delicious, peaches are full of healthy vitamins and minerals. They are most often eaten raw as a fruit, but are also used in pies and peach cobblers, and made into jelly.

HEIGHT: 10–15 ft.

FOUND IN: Sunny areas with well-drained soils

SEASON: Flowers in early spring; fruits harvested in summer

SPARKLEBERRY
(Vaccinium arboreum)

Sparkleberry is closely related to the blueberry and cranberry, and grows as a shrub. It is one of the earlier plants to flower each year and is an important source of early season nectar for many pollinators. The plant produces a lot of berries, which are eaten by many different animals.

Unlike other trees and shrubs, sparkleberry can be either deciduous or evergreen. Sparkleberry plants that live in areas with cold winters tend to be deciduous, but elsewhere they are evergreen.

HEIGHT: 7–12 ft. (shrub); up to 25 ft. (tree)

SEASON: Flowers in the spring; fruits start late summer and can remain on the plant through the winter

FOUND IN: A wide range of settings, most commonly in rocky and/or sandy woodlands

CROSSVINE
(Bignonia capreolata)

Crossvine is a woody vine that can grow as long as 50 feet. It is a very strong climber, and can grow up and over all kinds of surfaces, such as stone walls, fences, and the sides of houses. This, and the fact these vines attract hummingbirds, is why many people plant them in their yards. Hummingbirds are the main pollinators of crossvine, and love to feed from the flowers.

HEIGHT: Up to 50 ft. along the ground or up vertical surfaces

SEASON: Flowers from mid-spring through late summer; leaves at the tallest portions of the vines remain year-round, though they change color to a reddish-purple in the winter

FOUND IN: A wide range of conditions, from woodlands to swamps to roadsides and more

Georgia

NORTH AMERICAN RIVER OTTER
(Lontra canadensis)

SIZE: 3–5 ft.; males are larger than females

DIET: Fish, crayfish, amphibians, reptiles, bird eggs, and aquatic plants

FOUND IN: Almost any type of freshwater wetland with ample food

The North American river otter is a member of the weasel family. These otters spend most of their time in the water. All four of their feet are webbed, making them excellent swimmers. They can close their nostrils and ears underwater, where they can stay for up to four minutes when diving for food.

When on land, North American river otters sometimes slide on their bellies, often in mud or snow. This helps them travel overland between wetlands, and sometimes they seem to slide just for fun!

GREEN HERON
(Butorides virescens)

The green heron is one of the smallest herons in the U.S.—about the size of a large crow. These herons will actively fish for food. They start do by dropping something small in the water—a feather, a piece of a leaf, a twig, or an insect. They then wait for it to attract fish for them to catch. They stay very still when doing this, and their color patterns help them blend in so they aren't seen.

SIZE: 1.5 ft. long; 2 ft. wingspan

FOUND IN: Wetlands

DIET: Mostly fish

GOPHER TORTOISE
(Gopherus polyphemus)

The gopher tortoise is the only tortoise in the eastern U.S. It spends most of its life underground in burrows that it digs. These burrows are usually about 15 feet long and up to 7 feet deep. The burrows provide gopher tortoises with a cool and moist place to live, and also help keep them safe from predators and during wildfires.

Many other wildlife species use gopher tortoise burrows—more than 350 that we know of! These include burrowing owls, indigo snakes, rabbits, and some frogs and toads.

SIZE: 1 ft. long

DIET: A wide range of low-growing plants

FOUND IN: Areas with sandy soils; also disturbed areas like pastures and urban areas

OSPREY
(Pandion haliaetus)

Ospreys spend much of their time near water. This is because they mostly eat fish, which they hunt for by soaring in circles over shallow water. When they see a fish, they dive after it feet-first and grab it with their very sharp talons.

Osprey populations declined drastically between 1945 and 1970. This was due to a chemical called DDT, which humans used to spray to control mosquitoes. When scientists figured out that DDT was affecting bird populations, it was banned in the U.S. Osprey populations have recovered well since then.

SIZE: 2 ft. long; 5 ft. wingspan

EGGS: Mainly fish

FOUND IN: Areas near large bodies of fresh and salt water

HAWAII

Hawaii is made up of eight large volcanic islands and a large number of smaller islands, called "islets." Though it is the least biodiverse state in the U.S., it has the second-highest number of endemic species (species found nowhere else in the world). This is because it is so isolated in the middle of the Pacific Ocean, about 2,500 miles away from the closest point of land in California!

YELLOW HAWAIIAN HIBISCUS
(Hibiscus brackenridgei)

The yellow Hawaiian hibiscus is the state flower of Hawaii. This plant can grow either as a shrub or as a tree, depending on conditions.

The yellow Hawaiian hibiscus is only found in Hawaii, and even there is very rare. It is currently an endangered species, having declined dramatically over the past hundred years. One reason for this is the introduction of pigs, goats, deer, and cattle to Hawaii. These non-native animals feed on the Hibiscus plant, destroying its chance to thrive.

HEIGHT: 6–10 ft. (shrub); 15–30 ft. (tree)

FOUND IN: Lowland dry forests with ample sunlight

SEASON: Most commonly flowers in spring but can flower any time of the year

CANDLENUT TREE (KUKUI)
(Aleurites moluccanus)

The candlenut tree (also called the "kukui") is the state tree of Hawaii, but is not native to the state. It was brought to Hawaii over 1,000 years ago by Polynesian voyagers, who burned the oil that comes from its nuts to light lamps. This is how the tree got the name "candlenut."

The kukui tree has proven itself very useful over the years: the wood has been used to build canoes, and the sap to make clothes waterproof. A variety of medicines have been made from its roots.

HEIGHT: 50–70 ft.

FOUND IN: Most common in moist lowland forests

SEASON: Most commonly flowers in spring but can have flowers any time of year; keeps leaves year-round

BEACH MORNING GLORY
(Ipomoea pes-caprae)

The beach morning glory grows like a vine along the upper edges of beaches and in coastal sand dunes. Luckily, it is very tolerant of dry, windy, and salty conditions. Each vine can grow as long as 15 feet. Because it grows as a wide, sprawling mat on top of the sand, it is very important for controlling erosion (stopping the sand from slipping away).

Some surfers have a special connection to beach morning glory. There is a legend that slapping the vine on top of the water will create better surfing waves.

HEIGHT: Grows low along the ground

FOUND IN: The upper edges of beaches and in sand dunes

SEASON: Flowers and keeps leaves year-round

ʻŌHELO ʻAI
(Vaccinium reticulatum)

The ʻōhelo ʻai is a low shrub found only in Hawaii. It produces berries related to cranberries and blueberries. These come in a wide range of colors, including red, purple, blue, black, and yellow. ʻŌhelo ʻai berries are an important food source for the nēnē, and their seeds are spread in its droppings.

The ʻōhelo ʻai is adapted to grow on recent lava flows. It can even survive being partially buried by ash fall.

HEIGHT: Typically less than 3 ft.

FOUND IN: High elevations on recent lava flows and freshly disturbed volcanic ash

SEASON: Flowers any time of year but mostly early spring through summer; fruits are most prevalent throughout the summer

HAWAII

LAYSAN ALBATROSS
(Phoebastria immutabilis)

Laysan albatrosses are very large seabirds, with a wingspan of about 6 feet. They are incredibly skilled fliers and can glide in the air over the ocean for hours at a time without flapping their wings even once. They spend about half of the year in the open ocean and the other half of the year on islands raising their young.

The Laysan albatross is one of the oldest-living birds in the world, living for fifty years or more. The most famous wild Laysan albatross is a female named Wisdom, who lives on Midway Island in Hawaii. As of 2024, Wisdom was at least seventy-three years old and had successfully raised at least thirty chicks. Scientists estimate that Wisdom has flown at least three million miles over her lifetime. That is roughly the equivalent of circling the entire Earth 120 times, or taking six trips to the moon and back!

SIZE: 2.5 ft. long; 6.5 ft. wingspan

FOUND IN: Open ocean and breeding islands

DIET: Squid, fish, and barnacles

NĒNĒ (HAWAIIAN GOOSE)
(Branta sandvicensis)

The nēnē, also known as the "Hawaiian goose," is the state bird of Hawaii and only found on the Hawaiian Islands.

The nēnē is an endangered species, currently the rarest goose in the world. This is mainly due to the introduction of mammals, like mongooses, rats, and pigs, to the Hawaiian Islands, which prey on the geese as well as their eggs. Thanks to a lot of work by scientists and conservation organizations, however, nēnē populations are growing.

SIZE: 2 ft. long; 3 ft. wingspan

FOUND IN: High-elevation grasslands, shrublands, and lava flows

DIET: A wide range of plants, seeds, and fruits

GREEN SEA TURTLE (HONU)

(Chelonia mydas)

The green sea turtle, or the "honu" in Hawaiian, is the most seen sea turtle in Hawaii, often spotted when people are snorkeling.

Hawaiian green sea turtles don't reach adulthood until they are twenty-five to forty years old. Once they do, the females will start to reproduce. Each chooses a nesting beach and lays their eggs on that same beach every two to five years. Green sea turtles can live for sixty to seventy years, almost the entirety of which is spent in the ocean.

SIZE: 4 ft. long

EGGS: The female mates every 2–5 years, laying up to 500 eggs each time

FOUND IN: Oceans in tropical and temperate regions around the world

Idaho

Idaho is made up of a mix of dry grasslands, shrub basins and plains, rivers and river valleys, and mountains. Each of these habitats contains its unique set of plant and animal communities adapted to the conditions there. Much of the state is undeveloped and quite remote, so many animals rarely, if ever, come into contact with humans in Idaho.

WESTERN WHITE PINE
(Pinus monticola)

The western white pine is the state tree of Idaho. It can grow to be very large—often over 100 feet tall, and sometimes almost 200 feet. It can live for 300 to 500 years.

Western white pines used to be very abundant in northern Idaho, but have declined dramatically due to a fungus called "white pine blister rust." This fungus was accidentally introduced to the U.S. from Europe in 1909. In some areas of Idaho, it has killed more than ninety percent of western white pine trees.

HEIGHT: 100–175 ft.

SEASON: Retains needles year-round; cones drop in the fall

FOUND IN: Variable settings ranging from moist valleys to relatively high-elevation mountain slopes

WESTERN REDCEDAR
(Thuja plicata)

The western redcedar is a tree with a very long lifespan. Some live more than 1,000 years. Their wood is very resistant to rotting, so they can thrive in wet areas. This also lends the wood to being used for roof shingles and for siding on houses.

Many different animals take cover in the cavities of western redcedars, including bears, raccoons, skunks, and various birds. Western redcedar saplings' foliage is also vital winter food for elk and deer.

HEIGHT: 100–150 ft.

SEASON: Retains needles year-round

FOUND IN: Cool and moist habitats regardless of elevation

RED ELDERBERRY
(Sambucus racemosa)

Red elderberry grows as a large tree-like shrub, and produces many tiny red berries. If eaten raw, these berries are poisonous to humans. Many indigenous communities would steam them first, and then store them for winter food. They would also use other parts of the plant to make a range of medicines.

Unlike humans, many animals can eat the raw fruits of red elderberry without being harmed. Lots of pollinators also feed on nectar from its flowers, including hummingbirds, butterflies, bees, and flies.

HEIGHT: 8–12 ft. (shrub); up to 20 ft. (tree)

FOUND IN: Moist to wet areas

SEASON: Flowers in early spring; fruits in summer; drops leaves for the winter

STICKY GERANIUM
(Geranium viscosissimum)

The sticky geranium is a flower of the rose family. It produces bright pink to purple flowers that bloom all summer. This plant is so-called because its leaves have a sticky substance on them that helps trap insects, which the plant then digests.

The flowers of sticky geranium are edible by people and are sometimes put in salads. Sticky geranium is often planted in yards for ornamental reasons. It is popular because it needs little water, thrives both in sun and partial shade, and blooms for a long time each year.

HEIGHT: 1.5–3 ft.

SEASON: Flowers from late spring to mid-/late summer

FOUND IN: A wide range of settings and elevations such as forests, grasslands, and high-elevation meadows

Idaho

ELK
(Cervus canadensis)

Elk are the second-largest member of the deer family (moose are the largest). Elk live in herds, which are sometimes made up of as many as 300–400 individuals. Adult males, known as "bulls," and adult females, known as "cows," have their own separate herds, except during the breeding season.

In the breeding season, bull elk compete with one another to win the right to mate with cow elk. Bulls with the biggest antlers and deepest bugle calls will often win these competitions without the need for an altercation. Sometimes, however, they will challenge each other physically. When this happens, the two bulls will lock their antlers and push each other back and forth as a test of strength. The loser of this battle will move on in search of other potential mates.

SIZE: 6.5 ft. long (females); 8 ft. long (males)

DIET: Grasses, shrubs, and tree bark

FOUND IN: A wide variety of habitats, from alpine meadows to forests and wetlands

RUFOUS HUMMINGBIRD
(Selasphorus rufus)

Rufous hummingbirds expend a lot of daily energy on flying. In a single day, some visit upwards of 1,000 flowers to refuel on their nectar, and may consume up to three times their own weight in food.

Rufous hummingbirds are well known for their feisty personalities. They will often chase away other birds they perceive as competitors for food, including birds much bigger than they are.

SIZE: 3–3.5 in. long; 4.5 in. wingspan

DIET: Nectar from a variety of flowers; also insects and spiders

FOUND IN: Almost any type of habitat, ranging from parks to shrublands, wetlands, and forests

WESTERN FENCE LIZARD

(Sceloporus occidentalis)

The western fence lizard is so-called because it often basks on fences. It can also be found on logs, rocks, and the branches of shrubs, where its body coloration and patterning help it to blend in.

You can easily tell a male western fence lizard apart from a female: Males have a large bright-blue patch on each side of their belly and throat, which they use in territorial displays with other males, and to attract females.

SIZE: 6–7 in. long (including tail)

EGGS: The female lays an average of 8 eggs per year

FOUND IN: Open areas containing some shrubs, and with a lot of wood and rocks on the ground

BOLD JUMPING SPIDER

(Phidippus audax)

The bold jumping spider is one of about 300 U.S. species of jumping spider. They actively hunt for food, rather than building webs to catch prey like many other spiders do, though sometimes they will steal food from other spiders' webs.

Bold jumping spiders are active during the daytime, and at night they hide in small crevices and cavities. They are very cautious around animals larger than them and, because of this, they will often quickly flee if you approach.

SIZE: 0.25–0.5 in.

EGGS: The female lays about 200 eggs per year, guarding them until they hatch after about 1 month

FOUND IN: Open areas such as grasslands, prairies, old fields, gardens, and open woodlands

ILLINOIS

Illinois is one of the flatter states in the U.S. Its highest elevation is just over 1,200 feet above sea level. Much of the state is a mix of grasslands, agriculture, prairies, and forests, in addition to some moderate-sized rivers. In terms of biodiversity, Illinois is ranked in the middle of all fifty states.

SHAGBARK HICKORY
(Carya ovata)

The shagbark hickory tree can grow to over 100 feet tall and live to be more than 350 years old. It is so-called because of its "shaggy" bark. Some bats will roost under pieces of this bark during the summer.

Shagbark hickory trees produce a lot of nuts, which are eaten by humans as well as many other animals. These include squirrels, bears, raccoons, foxes, and chipmunks, as well as some birds, such as turkeys, bobwhite quails, and even ducks.

HEIGHT: 60–90 ft.

FOUND IN: A wide range of settings

SEASON: Flowers in mid-spring; nuts drop in early fall; drops leaves for the winter

RED COLUMBINE
(Aquilegia canadensis)

The red columbine produces beautiful red and yellow flowers. Unusually, these flowers are faced upside down, and each has five funnel-shaped, nectar-filled sepals. They are pollinated by hummingbirds, bumblebees, and some long-tongued insects. Hummingbirds have to plunge their whole heads into the flowers to get to the nectar!

Hardy, pretty, and attractive to hummingbirds, the red columbine is a favorite for gardens.

HEIGHT: 1–3 ft.

FOUND IN: Rocky woodlands, most commonly

SEASON: Flowers from mid-spring to early summer

COMMON MILKWEED
(Asclepias syriaca)

Common milkweed is very important for various insects. More than 400 insect species, including many different ants, flies, bees, wasps, beetles, and butterflies, have been documented feeding on it, mostly from its nectar.

Like other milkweed species, common milkweed is best known for its relationship with the monarch butterfly, which feeds on the leaves and uses their toxic properties to ward off predators. This protects them from birds and other potential predators.

In recent decades, milkweed has been declining in the U.S. Scientists think this is mainly due to the use of chemical herbicides as well as extensive mowing on roadsides and the edges of agricultural fields. This is bad news for monarch butterflies, as well as the other insects that depend on milkweed.

HEIGHT: 3–5 ft.

SEASON: Flowers most frequently in summer

FOUND IN: Open, sunny areas such as meadows, pastures, prairies, and roadsides

ILLINOIS

EASTERN CHIPMUNK
(Tamias striatus)

Eastern chipmunks spend most of their life underground in burrows. A chipmunk's burrow is complex, with multiple levels, and separate chambers for food storage and sleeping.

From spring to fall, eastern chipmunks spend a lot of time collecting food, which they store in the designated chambers of their burrows. By the start of winter, some will have stored more than a gallon of food to get them through the cold months.

SIZE: 3–4.5 in. long

DIET: A variety of nuts, seeds, and berries, as well as a range of insects

FOUND IN: Almost any natural or human-developed setting

AMERICAN GOLDFINCH
(Spinus tristis)

American goldfinches are regular visitors to backyard birdfeeders. They especially like feeders with thistle seeds. The males are a striking bright yellow with contrasting black-and-white wings. The females are a duller greenish-yellow, but are beautiful in their own right.

American goldfinches lay their eggs in the summer, much later in the year than most other birds. This is because they want to ensure that the seeds of their favorite plants, like thistle and milkweed, are available for their young to feed on.

SIZE: 5 in. long; 9 in. wingspan

DIET: Almost entirely seeds

FOUND IN: In and near meadows, parks, and yards containing wildflowers

EASTERN TIGER SALAMANDER
(Ambystoma tigrinum)

The eastern tiger salamander is one of the largest U.S. salamanders. They often grow to be a bit longer than an adult human's hand, and about the width of a whiteboard marker.

Eastern tiger salamanders live in burrows made by shrews, voles, and chipmunks. During the winter, they stay underground in their burrows, coming out only at night to hunt for food. In early spring, they then migrate to fishless ponds, where they breed and lay their eggs.

SIZE: 7–10 in.

EGGS: The female lays on average about 1,000 eggs per year

FOUND IN: Mainly woodlands, though also shrublands, prairies, and wetlands

PEARL CRESCENT
(Phyciodes tharos)

The pearl crescent is a small, brightly colored butterfly. Its name comes from the small, pearly-white, crescent-shaped markings on the underside of its back wings.

Pearl crescents are very active and will often chase other butterflies that enter their territory. Adult pearl crescents feed mainly on the nectar of asters, and they also lay their eggs on these plants. Planting asters in your yard is a great way to attract these butterflies!

SIZE: Just over 0.5 in. long; 1.25–1.75 in. wingspan

EGGS: The female lays an average of 35 eggs in a cluster on the underside of aster leaves

FOUND IN: Open areas such as grasslands, prairies, yards, and woodland openings

Indiana

Indiana is quite a flat state. The difference between the highest elevation in the state and the lowest elevation is just under 1,000 feet! This somewhat limits the biodiversity, though it is still relatively high thanks to the wide range of climate conditions as you go from north to south.

JACK-IN-THE-PULPIT
(Arisaema triphyllum)

This plant can be either male or female, with the female plant being known as a "Jill-in-the-pulpit." It has quite a fascinating pollination design: The flower sits inside a tall, narrow, cylindrical structure called the "pulpit," which has a hood. The flower lures its pollinators to the bottom of the pulpit with a special odor.

Sometimes, the fungus gnats that pollinate this plant get trapped at the bottom of the pulpit, and can only escape through a small hole found in the bottom. This hole is only present in the male plant. If a pollinator gets trapped in a female plant, there is no way out! The gnat will often die there, which maximizes the pollen available to fertilize the female flower.

HEIGHT: 1–2 ft.

SEASON: Flowers in spring

FOUND IN: Moist, shady woodlands and floodplains

BLACK CHERRY
(Prunus serotina)

Black cherry trees produce lots of delicious fruit, which is eaten by many different animals. These animals play an important role in dispersing the seeds inside of the fruits. In fact, seeds that pass through animals' digestive systems germinate better than those that do not.

The reddish-brown color and strength of black cherry wood makes it very popular for making furniture and cabinets.

HEIGHT: 50–80 ft.

SEASON: Flowers from late spring into early summer; fruits from summer into fall

FOUND IN: Sunny areas with rich soils, such as old fields and forest openings

AMERICAN TRUMPET VINE
(Campsis radicans)

The American trumpet vine is also known as the "trumpet creeper" and the "cow-itch vine." The "trumpet" part of the name comes from the shape of the flowers. Some people and animals may get mild redness and itchiness after contact with the leaves, which is where the name "cow-itch" comes from.

Ruby-throated hummingbirds often feed on the nectar of American trumpet vine flowers. In fact, they are one of its main pollinators. Another popular visitor is the sphinx moth—among the largest moths in the U.S.

HEIGHT: Each vine can grow up to about 30 ft. long

SEASON: Flowers in the summer for around 3 months

FOUND IN: Open areas such as thickets, roadsides, and fencerows; also along river banks and woodland openings

Indiana

RED FOX
(Vulpes vulpes)

The red fox is a very adaptable animal. It can live in a wide variety of landscape settings and eat a range of foods. Red foxes sometimes hide extra food by digging a hole and burying it to come back to at a later date.

Red foxes birth and raise their young in underground dens. These dens are located in tunnels that can be upwards of 20 feet long. Some are expansions on existing burrows made by foxes and other animals, like woodchucks and skunks.

SIZE: 2–3 ft. long

DIET: Small mammals, birds, amphibians and reptiles, invertebrates, and fruit

FOUND IN: Areas where forests abut fields, meadows, or orchards

NORTHERN CARDINAL
(Cardinalis cardinalis)

Male northern cardinals are brightly colored birds. They get their red coloration from the berries and fruits that they eat. The females are not as brightly colored as the males, but are quite beautiful nonetheless.

Northern cardinals are very territorial, especially the males during breeding season. They are often seen chasing away other northern cardinals that enter their territory. They will even attack their own reflections in car mirrors or other reflective surfaces, mistaking themselves for other birds!

SIZE: 9 in. long; 12 in. wingspan

DIET: Seeds, berries, and invertebrates

FOUND IN: Open woodlands, shrubby areas, yards, and parks

SOUTHERN TWO-LINED SALAMANDER
(Eurycea cirrigera)

The southern two-lined salamander is a type of stream salamander that spends most of its active season in and near streams and brooks. At night, it travels into nearby forests and feeds on the forest floor.

The female of this species lays her eggs under rocks or logs in the water, guarding them until they hatch. Hatchling salamanders live the first two years of their lives in the water, breathing via external gills. When they become adults, they breathe through their skin instead.

SIZE: 2.5–4 in.

FOUND IN: Streams, brooks, and seepages

EGGS: The female typically lays 20–50 (but sometimes up to 100) eggs under rocks or logs in streams

EASTERN PONDHAWK
(Erythemis simplicicollis)

The eastern pondhawk is a large dragonfly that hunts over and near ponds and other still bodies of water. These dragonflies are aggressive hunters, and sometimes prey on insects even bigger than themselves. Eastern pondhawks are often active from spring through the fall—a longer period than most other dragonflies.

The male and female of this species look quite different from one another. The male is bright blue all over, whereas the female has a bright green body, with a black, green, and white tail. Females are sometimes nicknamed "green jackets" because of this color pattern.

SIZE: 1.5–1.75 in. long; 2.5 in. wingspan

FOUND IN: Shorelines of almost any fairly open freshwater wetland

EGGS: The female lays up to 900 eggs in water

IOWA

Iowa is mostly farmland, plains, and prairie. Farmland makes up more than eighty-five percent of the total land area in the state. Because of the limited diversity of habitats, and limited area of natural environments, Iowa ranks in the bottom third of all states in terms of numbers of plant and animal species found there.

EASTERN BLACK WALNUT
(*Juglans nigra*)

The wood of the eastern black walnut tree is some of the most highly valued wood in the U.S. today. It is often used to make top-quality furniture. This is due to its beautiful dark color, straight grain, and strength.

Eastern black walnut is also extremely valuable to wildlife. Many animals eat the walnuts that fall from these trees, including chipmunks, squirrels, raccoons, turkeys, and bears. Walnut trees attract over a hundred types of caterpillar and moth, which, in turn, are a key food for many birds.

HEIGHT: 70–80 ft.

SEASON: Flowers in mid- to late spring; walnuts drop in early fall

FOUND IN: A wide range of settings, as long as there is abundant sunlight

PRICKLY WILD ROSE
(*Rosa acicularis*)

Prickly wild rose is a popular garden plant, as its flowers are both pretty to look at and nice to smell. These flowers have a long history of use in perfumes and teas, and are also an important nectar source for some beekeepers.

In the wild, many bird species nest in prickly wild rose bushes. The dense thorny thickets provided by this plant offer great protection from predators. The fruits of the prickly wild rose, called "rose hips," are loaded with vitamins. Lots of songbirds and mammals eat the rose hips as a result.

HEIGHT: 4–8 ft.

SEASON: Blooms late spring to early summer; fruits in late summer

FOUND IN: A wide range of settings, including thickets, wooded hillsides, and stream banks

WILD BLUE PHLOX
(Phlox divaricata)

Wild blue phlox, or "woodland phlox," adds color to shady woodlands and parts of fields. Interestingly, long-tongued insects are the only pollinators that can pollinate them. This is because the nectar is located at the base of a relatively long, thin tube at the center of the flowers. These long-tongued insects include some butterflies and bees (including bumblebees), as well as two types of moths (hummingbird clearwing and sphinx) that feed like hummingbirds.

HEIGHT: 1–1.5 ft.

SEASON: Flowers in mid- to late spring

FOUND IN: Open woodlands, partially shaded meadows, and along stream banks

MAYAPPLE
(Podophyllum peltatum)

Mayapple is an herbaceous plant that is typically found growing as a large, dense colony. It gets part of its name from the fruit it produces, which resembles a small apple. This fruit appears in the summer, not in May as the name might suggest. It is the single flower of each mayapple plant that appears in May.

Many different animals, including box turtles, eat this fruit. While some people do eat it too, it's probably safest not to. The entire plant, except for the fruit, is very toxic to people. Some of the toxins are contained in the seeds, but even if you remove these, the rest of the fruit can still make you ill.

HEIGHT: 1–2 ft.

SEASON: Flowers in April/May; fruits ripen throughout the summer

FOUND IN: Shady spots within a range of settings, including forests, fields, roadsides, and riverbanks

IOWA

COMMON RACCOON
(Procyon lotor)

Common raccoons excel at manipulating objects. They have very sensitive paws, with five dexterous toes on each of the front two paws. These allow them feel things very easily without having to see what they are holding.

Raccoons are great climbers, and spend a good amount of time in trees. The females often birth and raise young ("cubs") up in tree cavities, where they're safer from many predators.

SIZE: 2–3 ft. long

DIET: Extremely varied, including almost anything they can grab that is edible

FOUND IN: Almost any setting, including even the most developed urban areas

MALLARD
(Anas platyrhynchos)

The mallard is one of the most abundant ducks in the world. There are about 50 million in total, and around 10 million in North America alone. Unlike with many birds, female mallards are more vocal than males, and make the typical quacking sound people associate with ducks.

The male of this species attracts the female with his bright yellow bill. The brighter the color, the healthier the male. Female mallards then incubate and raise their young alone. Mallards start making sounds even when they're still in their eggs! The other unborn hatchlings listen, and then, using these sounds, all hatch at once.

SIZE: 2 ft. long; 3 ft. wingspan

FOUND IN: Almost any body of water, mostly fresh water

DIET: A wide range of plant matter

COMMON WATERSNAKE
(Nerodia sipedon)

The common watersnake, also called the "northern watersnake," is not venomous, though people sometimes confuse it with the cottonmouth snake, which is. Either way (as with most snakes), a watersnake won't bother you as long as you aren't bothering it.

Common watersnakes are great swimmers. They can capture their prey both on land and underwater, where they can stay for over an hour. They usually only do this, however, when they feel threatened by a predator. In the winter they often live underground or in old beaver lodges with other snakes. This keeps them warmer than if they were alone.

SIZE: 2–3.5 ft. long

FOUND IN: In and along the edges of a wide variety of freshwater wetlands

YOUNG: The female gives birth to 20–40 live young

Kansas

Just over eighty-five percent of the land area in Kansas is farmland, with the remainder mostly grassland and prairie. The state has only a relatively minor scattering of woodlands and wetlands, meaning habitat diversity is quite limited. Kansas only ranks thirty-seventh out of fifty states for the number of plant and animal species found there, despite ranking fifteenth for total land area!

EASTERN COTTONWOOD
(Populus deltoides)

The eastern cottonwood is the state tree of Kansas. These are fast-growing trees. Though they rarely live more than eighty years, they are often among the tallest in their area. They also have wide crowns, which make them popular trees for shade—they're often planted in campgrounds, picnic areas, and parks.

Cottonwoods are named for their seeds, which are spread in a cotton-like material produced by the tree. This helps the seeds get caught by the wind and disperse further. It also helps them to remain afloat in water, which helps even more with dispersal. When eastern cottonwoods drop their seeds in late spring, it can seem like it is snowing!

HEIGHT: Average 75–100 ft., but can grow to over 150 ft.

FOUND IN: Floodplains and along rivers

SEASON: Flowers in early spring; seeds fall in late spring

ROUGHLEAF DOGWOOD
(Cornus drummondii)

While roughleaf dogwoods can grow as small trees, they often grow as dense, clumping shrubs in the wild. This creates a great protective structure that many birds like to nest in. They also produce lots of berries for birds and small mammals to feed on. All of this makes them a popular choice for wildlife-friendly yards.

Roughleaf dogwoods are also very hardy and can grow in locations that get very little water and sunlight.

HEIGHT: 10–15 ft.

FOUND IN: Almost any natural setting, though it does best in moist soils

SEASON: Flowers during the summer; fruits ripen in early fall

COMMON SUNFLOWER
(Helianthus annuus)

The common sunflower is the state flower of Kansas, and is known for its very large and striking flower heads. Many people plant these flowers in their yards.

Sunflowers are also grown commercially for their seeds. Sunflower seeds are a popular source of nutrition for humans, as well as a common seed for bird feeders. They are also the source of sunflower oil, used for cooking.

HEIGHT: Usually 5–10 ft., though sometimes much taller

FOUND IN: Open areas such as grasslands, meadows, prairies, and roadsides

SEASON: Blooms throughout the summer

BUTTERFLY MILKWEED
(Asclepias tuberosa)

The butterfly milkweed is one of seventy native U.S. milkweeds. Monarch butterflies use about half of these, including the butterfly milkweed, to lay their eggs on and for their caterpillars to feed on. Eating milkweed leaves makes the monarch caterpillars, and the butterflies they turn into, toxic.

Butterfly milkweed has beautiful orange flowers. These are an important source of nectar for a wide range of pollinators. These include many bees, flies, butterflies, moths, and even hummingbirds.

HEIGHT: 1.5–3 ft.

FOUND IN: A wide range of open settings

SEASON: Blooms throughout the summer

Kansas

EASTERN COTTONTAIL
(Sylvilagus floridanus)

The eastern cottontail, often referred to as the "cottontail rabbit," is found throughout the eastern half of the U.S. These are commonly seen in people's yards, especially during the warmer months of the year.

Female cottontails typically have up to four litters of young each year. The female makes a nest by digging out a shallow depression in the ground, which she lines with dried grass and fur that she pulls from her body. She visits the nest only at dawn and dusk, when she goes to nurse the young. The rest of the time, she stays away so not to attract predators to the nest.

SIZE: 14–18 in. long

DIET: A wide range of herbaceous plants and grasses; the stems and buds of woody plants in winter

FOUND IN: Open areas like fields, meadows, orchards, and yards

WESTERN MEADOWLARK
(Sturnella neglecta)

As their name suggests, western meadowlarks live in meadows and similar settings. The females of the species build their nests on the ground in areas of dense grass by weaving long grass stems together. These nests are dome-like structures, each with an entrance on the side. There are often narrow trails through the grass that lead to the nest—these are known as runways.

SIZE: 9 in. long; 16 in. wingspan

DIET: Insects, seeds, and grain

FOUND IN: Grasslands, pastures, and meadows

RING-NECKED SNAKE
(Diadophis punctatus)

The ring-necked snake is named for the orange ring around its neck, which matches its bright-orange underside. Sometimes, these snakes will flip their bodies to scare off predators with their lurid color.

Despite being among the most common snakes in their area, people don't often see ring-necked snakes. This is because they are small and active mostly at night, spending much of their time under cover of rocks or logs, or in brush piles.

SIZE: 9–15 in. long and very slender

FOUND IN: Woodlands and more open settings

EGGS: The female lays 2–5 eggs under rocks, logs, or other such objects

YELLOW GARDEN SPIDER
(Argiope aurantia)

The yellow garden spider is often seen when at its web, which can be quite large, and is often found in very conspicuous areas with a lot of sun. Most people will notice the females, which are up to three times larger than males, and are bright yellow and black in color, whereas the males are brown.

The web of this spider has a highly visible zig-zag pattern running down its middle. Scientists think this decoration helps birds to avoid flying into it by accident.

SIZE: 0.75–1 in. (females)

FOUND IN: Sunny areas such as gardens, meadows, and fields

EGGS: The female lays between 400 and 1,000 eggs in a sac; spiderlings hatch in the fall but often don't emerge until following spring

KENTUCKY

Deciduous forests cover about half of the total land area in Kentucky. In fact, Kentucky has the second-highest diversity of hardwood tree species among all fifty states, behind only Florida. Farmland and grassland are the two other predominant habitat types in the state.

TULIP TREE
(Liriodendron tulipifera)

The tulip tree, or "yellow poplar," is the state tree of Kentucky. It is one of the tallest hardwoods in the eastern U.S., as it is both fast-growing and can live up to 300 years. These are quite attractive trees, with beautiful, tulip-like flowers, making them popular shade trees for parks, streets, and even large yards. They are also very popular commercially, largely for timber.

HEIGHT: Typically 80–120 ft., though they can grow taller

FOUND IN: Rolling hills and lower mountain slopes

SEASON: Flowers in spring

TALL GOLDENROD
(Solidago altissima)

Tall goldenrod, also called "late goldenrod," is the state flower of Kentucky. It is one of thirty-three native goldenrod species found throughout the state. It grows in clusters and blooms from late summer well into the fall. Its bright yellow flowers add great beauty to the fall landscapes where it grows. These flowers attract a variety of butterflies, bees, and other insects, for whom they are an important late-season nectar source. They tend to be quite abundant in the places where they're found, partly because they release chemicals that reduce the growth of other plants.

HEIGHT: 2–6 ft.

FOUND IN: Almost any open setting

SEASON: Flowers from late summer well into fall

WOODLAND STONECROP

(*Sedum ternatum*)

Woodland stonecrop is a common succulent plant in the eastern U.S. Succulents are often found in very dry areas like deserts, but woodland stonecrop is actually mostly found in moist areas, often in forest understories.

Woodland stonecrop also grows in rocky areas with little soil, sometimes on top of boulders. This is where it gets the "stone" part of its name from. The reason it can grow in these settings is because its succulent leaves retain moisture, so it doesn't depend on the soil for water.

HEIGHT: 4–6 in.

FOUND IN: A wide range of settings

SEASON: Flowers in spring

YARROW

(*Achillea millefolium*)

Yarrow is a tall herbaceous plant. Some people view it as a weed but, in fact, it is anything but that. Its large, pungent flowerhead is a nectar source for many insects, including various bees, flies, beetles, and butterflies.

Many cavity-nesting birds line their nests with yarrow. Researchers believe they do this because the aromatic chemicals exuded by the plant may repel nest parasites.

HEIGHT: 2.5–3 ft.

FOUND IN: Almost any open setting

SEASON: Flowers from late spring into early fall

KENTUCKY

BIG BROWN BAT
(Eptesicus fuscus)

The big brown bat is one of the most widespread of all bats in the United States. It can be found in almost any setting from remote forests to deserts, developed cities, and anywhere in between. In more wild settings, it mainly roosts under loose tree bark, but if it can, it will roost in structures like old barns or houses.

Female big brown bats form something called maternity colonies—groups that come together to raise their young. These can include as few as five females, or as many as 500!

SIZE: 4–5 in. long; 12–14 in. wingspan

FOUND IN: Almost any setting

DIET: Mostly beetles, though also a range of other flying insects such as moths and flies

RED-WINGED BLACKBIRD
(Agelaius phoeniceus)

Red-winged blackbirds are among the most common birds in the U.S. There are over 100 million of them. Many spend the winter in large flocks, made up of thousands of individual birds.

Red-winged blackbirds are one of the most conspicuous birds in the marshes and grasslands, where they breed in the spring and summer. You can often see the males perched atop tall vegetation, defending their territory. They do this by showing their bright red shoulder patches while singing their loud song. This song sounds like "konk-ra-leee!"

SIZE: 9 in. long; 13 in. wingspan

FOUND IN: Freshwater and saltwater marshes, meadows and grasslands

DIET: Mostly invertebrates; also seeds and berries

FIVE-LINED SKINK
(Plestidon fasciatus)

The five-lined skink is named for the five bright lines that run down its body and onto its tail. Females of the species keep this pattern for their entire lives, whereas males turn a more uniform brown/olive color when they become adults. The males do get slightly more colorful during the breeding season, when their heads turn an orange-red color to attract females.

Young five-lined skinks have a very bright blue tail. This is an adaptation to help them escape predators. If a predator catches it, the skink can drop its tail, which distracts the predator with its bright colors, letting the skink get away. Skinks can regrow their tails, but they grow back shorter, and a much duller gray color.

SIZE: 5–8.5 in. long

EGGS: The female lays 6–18 eggs in rodent burrows, under rocks, logs, bark, or other debris

FOUND IN: Open wooded areas with lots of debris on ground; also steep, rocky ledge areas

RED-SPOTTED PURPLE
(Limenitis arthemis)

The colorful red-spotted purple butterfly looks very similar to a pipevine swallowtail. The idea is to fool predators, who stay clear of the pipevine swallowtail because of its awful taste.

Not only is the red-spotted purple good at deceiving predators, its caterpillar also looks very similar to a bird dropping! No one wants to eat bird droppings, so if it's convincing enough, the caterpillar stays safe.

SIZE: 2.25–3.5 in. wingspan

EGGS: The female lays eggs on the leaf tips of a wide variety of trees

FOUND IN: Forests and woodlands, parks, and suburban settings

Louisiana

Louisiana is a very flat state. In fact, the highest elevation in the state is only 535 feet above sea level! Much of southern and eastern Louisiana is on a variety of plains and coastal plains, including a great diversity of wetlands. Most of northern Louisiana is wooded.

BALD CYPRESS
(Taxodium distichum)

The bald cypress is the state tree of Louisiana. It is a deciduous conifer tree, which is quite a rare combination. Instead of broad leaves, like most deciduous trees have, bald cypress trees have needle-like leaves. They drop these in the fall, and grow new ones in the spring. Bald cypress trees are also unique in that they can grow in the middle of swamps, often in standing water. They can be extremely long-lived—in 2019 researchers confirmed that one living bald cypress tree was 2,624 years old. That makes bald cypress the fifth-longest-living tree species alive today!

HEIGHT: Typically 60–100 ft., though they can grow much taller

FOUND IN: Wet, swampy areas

SEASON: Drops needle-like leaves in the fall

LYRELEAF SAGE
(Salvia lyrata)

Lyreleaf sage is a very hardy plant. It can grow in a wide range of conditions and survive both flooding and drought. Its flowers are very attractive to hummingbirds and butterflies. As a result, it is commonly planted in gardens, especially by hummingbird enthusiasts.

The flowers of the lyreleaf sage are primarily pollinated by bees. The lower lip of these flowers is designed like a landing platform for bees. When the bees land, they get showered with pollen from inside the flower.

HEIGHT: 1–2 ft.

SEASON: Blooms from mid-spring to early summer

FOUND IN: A wide range of settings, including roadsides, fields, and open woodlands

PEPPERVINE
(Nekemias arborea)

Peppervine is a fast-growing vine. It can grow upwards of 35 feet, climbing tall tree trunks and becoming quite bushy. This vine mainly grows along stream- and riverbanks. Its roots can help stabilize the banks and reduce erosion.

Peppervine produces many berries, which are eaten by songbirds and mammals. They're not very tasty to humans, though, and can give some people an upset stomach. Some people use the peppervine stems to weave baskets from.

HEIGHT: Vines can grow upwards of 35 ft.

FOUND IN: A wide range of moist soil settings

SEASON: Flowers from late spring into early fall; fruits in early fall

PALE PITCHER PLANT
(Sarracenia alata)

The pale pitcher plant, also known the "yellow trumpet," is a carnivorous plant. This means it obtains some nutrients by trapping and consuming animals—primarily insects. As suggested by its name, this plant is shaped somewhat like a pitcher. It holds water in the bottom of this "pitcher," which contains digestive chemicals. Red lines lead down into the water, which some insects are known to follow. Once the insects enter this water they can't escape, and are digested by the plant.

HEIGHT: 1.5–2 ft.

FOUND IN: Marshes, bogs, and openings of forests with acidic soils

SEASON: Flowers from spring into early fall

Louisiana

NINE-BANDED ARMADILLO
(Dasypus novemcinctus)

The name "armadillo" means "little armored one" in Spanish, referring to the armor-like plates that cover much of this creature's body. These protect the armadillo against predators like mountain lions, black bears, and alligators.

Nine-banded armadillos are mainly active at night, when they are feeding. If they come across a river, they can walk across the bottom while holding their breath for over five minutes! Unfortunately, when it comes to crossing roads, many are killed by passing traffic. This is partly due to the armadillo's habit of jumping up when startled, which often causes it to hit the undersides of vehicles.

SIZE: 15–18 in. long, with a nearly equal-length tail

DIET: Mainly invertebrates, of a wide variety

FOUND IN: A wide range of habitats such as woodlands, wetlands, shrublands, and grasslands

BROWN PELICAN
(Pelecanus occidentalis)

The brown pelican has an exceptionally long bill with an expandable pouch. It uses this to catch fish by diving after them from the air. Before eating the fish, it tilts its head down to drain the water from inside the bill.

In the mid-1900s, brown pelicans nearly went extinct throughout much of their range. This was because of a pesticide called DDT, which was sprayed on crops to control mosquitoes. Fortunately, scientists discovered the pesticide's harmful effects on many animals and it was banned in 1972. Brown pelican populations have recovered well since then.

SIZE: 3–4.5 ft. long; 6.5 ft. wingspan

FOUND IN: Nearshore coastal settings

DIET: Mainly fish, of a wide variety

AMERICAN ALLIGATOR
(Alligator mississippiensis)

The American alligator is the second-largest reptile in the United States, second only to the American crocodile. American alligators are very powerful animals. They have strong tails that they use to swim effortlessly through water, and very powerful jaws that they use to catch their prey. Sometimes, when they catch especially large prey, they will drag it underwater to drown it.

Adult female alligators are very diligent mothers. After mating, the female will build a nest out of vegetation and soil to lay her eggs in. This can be up to 10 feet across and 3 feet tall, and is typically located on land near the edge of the water. After she's laid her eggs, she covers them up, and then guards the nest for the two months it takes for the eggs to hatch. When they are about to hatch, the young inside the eggs will make high-pitched noises. The mother hears this and removes the nesting material. She then carries the young safely to the water in her mouth, where they will stay with her for the next two to three years while they grow.

SIZE: Up to 9 ft. long (females); 12–14 ft. long (males)

FOUND IN: Freshwater marshes, swamps, lakes, canals, and slow-moving rivers

EGGS: The female lays 20–50 eggs in a nest

MAINE

Maine is a large and wild place. With over ninety percent of the state covered in forest, it is the most heavily forested state in the United States. Maine ranks fourth among states for length of coastline—nearly 3,500 miles of it. There are over 3,000 islands off the coast of Maine.

EASTERN WHITE PINE
(Pinus strobus)

The eastern white pine is the state tree of Maine. It is the largest conifer in most northeastern and upper-midwestern U.S. forests, where it is most common. It is heavily used by people as well as wildlife—its timber is very popular for construction and has long been used to build houses in the northeastern U.S. Many wildlife species eat the seeds of this pine, and use eastern white pine trees for nesting and shelter.

HEIGHT: 80–120 ft.

SEASON: Drops its cones in the fall

FOUND IN: A wide range of settings, though it does best in relatively dry soils

SHEEP LAUREL
(Kalmia angustifolia)

Sheep laurel is a low evergreen shrub that produces clusters of beautiful pink flowers. All parts of sheep laurel are extremely toxic if eaten by humans and other mammals, including sheep and cattle. This is how it gets its name, along with the nicknames "lamb kill" and "calf kill." The toxins in this plant help keep most animals from grazing on it.

Dense thickets of sheep laurel provide good winter cover for many birds. Some, especially ground-nesters, nest in it, including wild turkey, ruffed grouse, and willow ptarmigan.

HEIGHT: 1–3 ft.

SEASON: Flowers from late spring to early summer

FOUND IN: A wide range of settings, from bogs and swamps to dry pine forests

LOWBUSH BLUEBERRY
(Vaccinium angustifolium)

As its name suggests, lowbush blueberry grows low to the ground, and rarely exceeds 2 feet in height. Its "bushes" tend to look scraggly, often growing in sprawling clusters. Lowbush blueberry plants produce many berries, which are savored by people and wildlife alike.

Unlike many berry plants, lowbush blueberry prefers sandy, acidic soils. As a result, it is often associated with pine forests. It can even grow under full canopies, but the more sun it gets, the more berries it produces.

HEIGHT: 0.5–2 ft.

SEASON: Flowers in spring; fruits in mid- to late summer

FOUND IN: A range of open settings with sandy, acidic soils

LARGE-LEAVED LUPINE
(Lupinus polyphyllus)

Large-leaved lupine, or "bigleaf lupine," grows beautiful tall spikes of mostly purple flowers. These begin to flower in early to mid-spring and can bloom throughout the summer. The flowers provide vital nectar to many native bees, including bumblebees, while also attracting some hummingbirds and other pollinators.

Many people grow large-leaved lupine in their wildflower gardens, and plant nurseries have cultivated many different varieties for this purpose. These come in lots of different colors, from purples, reds, pinks, and yellows to whites and more.

HEIGHT: 2–5 ft.

SEASON: Flowers from mid-spring to mid-summer

FOUND IN: Areas of moist soil with adequate sun exposure

MAINE

SNOWSHOE HARE
(Lepus americanus)

Snowshoe hares are well adapted to the snowy areas where they live. They get their name because of their large hind feet, which help keep them on top of the snow. Each winter, these hares develop a nearly pure white coat, which helps them blend into the snowy landscape.

Hares and rabbits are closely related but have several notable differences: Hares tend to be larger and have bigger ears and longer legs than rabbits. If spotted by a predator, hares will flee quickly, while rabbits will try to stay still and rely on their camouflage. Finally, hares are born with fur and can run. Rabbits are born blind and hairless, and are relatively helpless animals.

SIZE: 18–20 in. long

DIET: A wide range of herbaceous plants and grasses; woody stems and tree bark in winter

FOUND IN: Mostly coniferous forests and coniferous-dominated swamps and bogs

ATLANTIC PUFFIN
(Fratercula arctica)

The Atlantic puffin is a small seabird that spends most of its life on the ocean. They only come ashore (on rocky islands and coastal cliffs) briefly each year to raise their young. Each pair lays a single egg in a burrow. The young puffin that hatches is known as a "puffling"!

Atlantic puffins are very skilled swimmers. They flap their wings underwater during hunting dives to propel themselves. They can dive as deep as 200 feet, though they often hunt in much shallower waters.

SIZE: 10–11 in. long; 1.5–2 ft. wingspan

DIET: A wide variety of small fish

FOUND: At sea, aside from in spring and summer when they raise their young on rocky islands and cliffs

WOOD TURTLE
(Glyptemys insculpta)

The wood turtle is different from most turtles in that it lives in rivers and streams. It will even overwinter there, either under the banks or sometimes on the bottom.

Wood turtles have a fascinating way of catching worms, which are one of their favorite food items. They lure the earthworms to the surface of the ground by stomping their front feet. Scientists think that this mimics the sound of moles underground, which are also worm predators. Worms then try to escape what they think is a mole by going above ground.

SIZE: 5–8 in. long

EGGS: The female lays 4–12 eggs in an underground nest she digs herself

FOUND IN: In and around slow-moving streams, brooks, and rivers

HUMMINGBIRD CLEARWING
(Hemaris thysbe)

The hummingbird clearwing is a beautiful moth, and fascinating to many people. Some people plant specific wildflowers in their yards to attract these moths, which look like very small hummingbirds. They even fly and hover like hummingbirds, and use a long proboscis, like a hummingbird's tongue, to feed on flower nectar. Unlike most moths (but like most butterflies), the hummingbird clearwing flies by day.

SIZE: 2 in. long; 1.5–2.25 in. wingspan

EGGS: The female lays her eggs on the underside of leaves

FOUND IN: Forest edges, meadows, and wildflower gardens

Maryland

Though Maryland ranks forty-second among the fifty states for total land area, it ranks twenty-eighth for number of combined plant and animal species. This is largely due to the range of diverse habitats there. There is abundance of coastal habitats in the east, and there are mountains in the west. Throughout, you will find a great deal of wooded and wetland habitats.

AMERICAN ELM
(Ulmus americana)

American elm trees used to be the main tree you'd find along downtown streets and in parks in many eastern U.S. towns and cities. They were popular for their fast growth, size, and intricate branches. They provide great shade on hot, sunny days.

In the late 1920s, Dutch elm disease was accidentally introduced into the U.S. from Europe. This disease spread quickly through the eastern U.S. and killed tens of millions of elms, including many that lined urban streets. American elms still exist in much of the eastern U.S. and Canada, but they are now much less common.

HEIGHT: 60–80 ft.

SEASON: Flowers in early spring

FOUND IN: Areas of moist soil, and quite frequently nearby wetlands

EASTERN REDBUD
(Cercis canadensis)

The eastern redbud produces stunning, magenta-pink flowers in the spring. The flowers often bloom before the leaves emerge, causing the entire crown of the tree to be ablaze in bright pink. People plant these trees in yards, along streets, and in parks due to their beautiful blooms. Some towns and cities have events centered around them. For example, Columbus, Wisconsin, is known as "Redbud City" and celebrates "Redbud Day" on a Saturday each May.

HEIGHT: 20–30 ft.

SEASON: Flowers in mid-spring

FOUND IN: A range of settings, but does best in open areas with moist, rich soils

BLACK-EYED SUSAN
(Rudbeckia hirta)

The black-eyed Susan is the state flower of Maryland. Its name refers to the dark brown center of the bright-yellow flower head. These tall flowers bloom for a long time, often throughout much of the summer and into early fall. Their beauty and hardiness make them popular in wildflower gardens. Many pollinators are attracted to their nectar, and a number of songbirds eat their seeds, most notably American goldfinches.

HEIGHT: 1.5–3 ft.

FOUND IN: A wide range of open and sunny settings

SEASON: Flowers from mid-summer into mid-fall

SHOWY ORCHID
(Galearis spectabilis)

The showy orchid is a low-growing and subtly beautiful flower found in deciduous woodlands. It blooms in early to mid-spring, often before the trees overhead have fully leafed out. This allows it to get some sunlight.

Showy orchids are quite rare, and in some states are even listed as an endangered species. This is mainly because they have very strict habitat requirements, but also because some people dig up wild orchids to plant in their gardens, which they shouldn't!

HEIGHT: 6–8 in.

FOUND IN: Moist, shady settings, often near streams and seasonal wetlands

SEASON: Flowers from late spring to early summer

Maryland

MUSKRAT
(Ondatra zibethicus)

The muskrat lives a similar existence to the beaver, with the exception that it doesn't build dams. Muskrats often live in small lodges in water, which they build from soft vegetation. Inside these lodges, they live in dry nesting chambers above the surface of the water, but accessed via underwater entrances. Muskrats sometimes also live in abandoned beaver lodges.

Muskrats swim primarily at the water's surface, but dive underwater if they sense a predator is nearby and can stay there for up to twenty minutes. Their partially webbed hind feet help them to swim, and their tails help them steer.

SIZE: 12 in. long

DIET: Stems and roots of aquatic vegetation as well as aquatic invertebrates (especially crayfish) and dead fish

FOUND IN: Almost any freshwater wetland type, especially those with cattails

BALTIMORE ORIOLE
(Icterus galbula)

Male Baltimore orioles have stunning orange-colored bodies, black heads, and black feathers on their wings and tail. The female is a bit more of a dull orange color, but is beautiful in her own right. She is also a very talented nest-builder, constructing a woven basket-like pouch that hangs from the end of a tree branch. To make this nest, she must weave thousands of stitches from vegetation.

To attract Baltimore orioles to your yard, put out fruit. In particular, these birds like dark fruits that are ripe. Oranges cut in half and dark jellies (such as grape or raspberry) are the best for attracting them.

SIZE: 9 in. long; 12 in. wingspan

DIET: Invertebrates, berries, and nectar

FOUND IN: Open deciduous woodlands, woodland edges, and deciduous trees in meadows and pastures

DIAMONDBACK TERRAPIN
(Malaclemys terrapin)

The diamondback terrapin is the only turtle in the U.S. that lives in brackish water—water that is part salt, but not as salty as pure seawater. They can survive in this water because they have glands that remove the extra salt through tears that come from their eyes!

Terrapins are primarily carnivores, and mostly eat shelled animals, such as crabs, snails, clams, and mussels. They have powerful jaws and crushing plates in their mouths, which help them break down the shells.

SIZE: 11 in. long (females); 5 in. long (males)

FOUND IN: Salt marshes, tidal creeks, and estuaries

EGGS: The female lays 4–18 eggs in an underground nest, which she digs herself

EASTERN TIGER SWALLOWTAIL
(Papilio glaucus)

The eastern tiger swallowtail is a yellow butterfly with black stripes, which is how it gets the "tiger" part of its name. In most of the areas where it is found, it is one of the largest butterflies around. It is one of over 500 swallowtail species worldwide.

Groups of males are sometimes seen "puddling." This is when a large number gather at puddles or muddy spots on the ground to ingest important compounds, such as sodium, which help them with breeding.

SIZE: 2 in. long; 3–5.5 in. wingspan

FOUND IN: Almost any setting where deciduous trees are present

EGGS: The female lays eggs on the leaves of various host trees

MASSACHUSETTS

The types of habitats in Massachusetts change a great deal as you go from east to west. Eastern Massachusetts has extensive and diverse coastal habitats, and as you move westward, the state is covered in a variety of forests. The western third of the state also rises steeply in elevation. As a result, the plants and animals you encounter in Massachusetts can be quite different, depending where you are in the state.

EASTERN RED CEDAR
(Juniperus virginiana)

The eastern red cedar is a relatively small evergreen tree. It grows in a somewhat pyramidal shape when young, but gets rounder as it ages. It can often live for over 300 years. The oldest reported eastern red cedar was over 900 years old.

The eastern red cedar is important for many animals. Its combination of dense branches and year-round foliage attracts many songbirds, which nest in it and use it for cover. A variety of mammals and birds gorge themselves on its abundant and nutrient-packed fruits.

HEIGHT: 40–50 ft.

FOUND IN: Dry, exposed sites

SEASON: Fruits (on female plants only) ripen in the fall and remain on the tree through winter

HIGHBUSH BLUEBERRY
(Vaccinium corymbosum)

The highbush blueberry plant gets part of its name because of how tall it grows. Less sparse than a "bush," it is better described as a "shrub," and is one of about thirty-five blueberry species that grow wild in the U.S.

Highbush blueberry plants produce vast amounts of large blueberries, which typically fruit in the summer. They are a favorite food for many birds and mammals, and for thousands of years have been a staple in our diets.

HEIGHT: 6–12 ft.

FOUND IN: Moist edges of wetlands; also dry sites with sandy, acidic soils

SEASON: Fruits ripen in summer

NEW ENGLAND ASTER
(Symphyotrichum novae-angliae)

New England aster flowers bloom in late summer and fall, bringing a stunning deep purple to the landscapes where they're found. Each plant has fifty to a hundred flower heads (sometimes even more), and each flower has up to a hundred thin, deep-purple rays that extend from a yellow circular eye at the center. These plants often grow in dense colonies. Their flowers, besides being beautiful, provide nectar to late-season pollinators and food for monarch butterflies during their late-summer migrations.

HEIGHT: 3–5 ft.

SEASON: Flowers from late summer to late fall

FOUND IN: A wide range of settings, as long as there is adequate sun exposure

TRAILING ARBUTUS
(Epigaea repens)

Trailing arbutus, also commonly called "mayflower," is the state flower of Massachusetts, and grows sprawling (or "trailing") along the ground. Its leaves are evergreen, yet its flowers only bloom very briefly in the spring. Its flowers are known for their magnificent, sweet smell, which used to make them very popular for people to dig up and try to plant in their own yards. This used to happen so much that the state of Massachusetts passed a law fining anyone who does this.

HEIGHT: 4–6 in.

SEASON: Flowers for a short period in spring

FOUND IN: Dry, sandy soils, often growing under conifers

MASSACHUSETTS

WOODCHUCK
(Marmota monax)

The woodchuck is also commonly referred to as a "groundhog." It doesn't chuck wood, as its name might suggest. In fact, it gets its name from the Cree word "wuchak," which refers to other similar-looking species, including the fisher and the weasel.

Woodchucks live much of their lives in burrows. They have summer burrows, which are usually located in open areas such as fields, meadows, and pastures, and often have multiple entrances and chambers. These can be up to 45 feet long. To hibernate, woodchucks go to a winter burrow, which tends to be in a more wooded setting. Before beginning their hibernation, they close all the entrances.

SIZE: 1.5–2 ft. long

DIET: A very wide variety of vegetation

FOUND IN: Open areas such as fields, meadows, orchards, and open woodlands

AMERICAN ROBIN
(Turdus migratorius)

American robins will be very familiar to people living in suburban areas, where they can be seen searching for worms in people's lawns. To find these worms, they rely primarily on sight, looking for very fine movements in the soil and grass. The robin will often tilt its head when doing this to get a better view, because its eyes are on the sides of its head.

During the winter, robins eat mostly fruits and berries. In late winter, some American robins behave like they are a bit drunk. This is from having eaten over-ripe berries that have fermented to create alcohol!

SIZE: 10 in. long; 17 in. wingspan

DIET: Mostly insects, berries, and worms

FOUND IN: Forests, woodlands and forest edges, shrublands, yards, and parks

EASTERN GARTER SNAKE
(Thamnophis sirtalis)

Garter snakes are named for their striped patterns, which look like sock garters. People often mishear the name as "garden snake," and the fact that they're often encountered in people's gardens only adds to this confusion.

Garter snakes are more cold-tolerant than many other snakes. This means they can be active earlier in the spring and later in the fall. In the winter, they hibernate together in large groups, which can number into the hundreds (and in some locations even more than that!). This helps them keep much warmer than if they hibernated alone.

SIZE: 18–32 in. long

FOUND IN: Essentially any habitat setting

YOUNG: The female gives live birth to 15–40 young

WOOLLY BEAR
(Pyrrharctia isabella)

The woolly bear is the caterpillar of the Isabella tiger moth. This large orange and black caterpillar is at the center of a long-held myth: that the blacker the caterpillars, the more severe the winter ahead will be. You can't actually predict the winter based on their color pattern.

Woolly bears are commonly seen during the fall, when many are encountered crossing roads as they travel to find a place to overwinter. This will usually be the inside of a log, in thick brush piles, or under bark. After the caterpillars have hibernated, they transform into an adult Isabella tiger moths the following spring or early summer.

SIZE: 1.5–2 in.

FOUND IN: Marshes and meadows (and nearby areas)

Michigan

Michigan is roughly fifty percent forested and twenty-five percent farmland, with the remainder spread across a range of cover types. Though inland, Michigan ranks ninth among states for total coastline, and first for total freshwater wetland coastline. This is due to its having coastlines along four of the Great Lakes.

JACK PINE
(Pinus banksiana)

The jack pine is a hardy pine tree that typically grows soon after forest fires. It is most prevalent in the upper Midwest and extends further north in Canada than any other American pine tree.

Jack pine is important to a wide variety of wildlife. It is vital, for example, to the rare Kirtland's warbler. This bird was once endangered (though it was delisted in 2019), and only breeds in young jack pine forests. Widespread, historic declines in jack pine, due to logging and fire suppression, nearly drove the Kirtland's warbler to extinction.

HEIGHT: 40–60 ft.

FOUND IN: Sandy, acidic soils

SEASON: Retains individual cones for upwards of 10 years

DWARF LAKE IRIS
(Iris lacustris)

The dwarf lake iris is the state flower of Michigan. Since 1988, the U.S. Fish and Wildlife Service has listed it as a federally threatened species. It has a very limited distribution in the U.S., where it occurs only along the northern shores of Lakes Huron and Michigan.

Dwarf lake iris grows low to the ground and has beautiful violet-blue flowers when in bloom.

HEIGHT: 4–6 in.

SEASON: Flowers from mid-May to early June

FOUND IN: Shallow soils along the shorelines of northern parts of Lakes Huron and Michigan

GHOST PIPE
(Monotropa uniflora)

The ghost pipe doesn't contain chlorophyll, which is why it is totally white, rather than having green parts. Most plant species use chlorophyll to convert energy from the sun into food, but the ghost pipe instead steals nutrients from the roots of nearby trees. It does this with the help of specific types of underground fungi. Nutrients flow in one direction from the tree's roots through the fungi and into the ghost pipe's roots. This is why you most often see the ghost pipe near the base of trees.

HEIGHT: 4–8 in.

FOUND IN: Moist, shady forests

SEASON: Flowers throughout the summer

SPOTTED JOE-PYE WEED
(Eutrochium maculatum)

Spotted joe-pye weed is a rather tall herbaceous flower. The "spotted" part of the name comes from the many purple spots that cover its stem. Another common name for this plant is "queen of the meadow."

When in bloom, each plant produces a wide cluster of pink or purple flower heads. These flowers are very attractive to a range of butterflies (especially skippers) and long-tongued bees, like bumblebees. Because of this, spotted joe-pye weed is often planted in wildflower gardens.

HEIGHT: 3–6 ft.

FOUND IN: Shallow, sun-exposed wetlands

SEASON: Flowers from mid-summer to early fall

Michigan

AMERICAN MARTEN
(Martes americana)

The American marten is a member of the weasel family. These creatures are agile climbers and spend much of their time up in trees, most often pines and firs. Even in places where they are quite abundant, they aren't often seen. This is mainly because they are solitary, tend to be quiet, and are active mostly at night.

American martens are great climbers and strong swimmers, and excel at traveling through snow. As winter approaches, they grow long hairs between their toepads, which help them to stay on top of the snow. They also are able to travel under snowpack quite well if they decide to do so.

SIZE: 14–17 in. long; males are slightly larger than females

FOUND IN: Mature forests that are mostly or entirely coniferous

DIET: Small mammals, insects, and berries

CANADA GOOSE
(Branta canadensis)

The Canada goose is aptly named—it breeds across almost all of Canada, except for the extreme north. It also breeds throughout much of the northern U.S. In winter, these geese are found throughout almost the entirety of the lower forty-eight states.

Canada geese mate for life, unless one of the pair dies. They raise their young, called "goslings," in a group with other pairs of Canada geese. These mixed groups of young are called "créches," which is a British word (borrowed from French) for "daycare."

SIZE: 2–4 ft. long; 3.5–5 ft. wingspan

FOUND IN: Wetlands with open water; they often feed in grassy fields

DIET: Aquatic vegetation, grasses, and other herbaceous plants; remnant corn and grains in harvested fields

EASTERN RED-BACKED SALAMANDER
(Plethodon cinereus)

The eastern red-backed salamander is one of the most abundant vertebrates where it lives. You often find these under decaying logs on the forest floor, or sometimes under rocks. They spend much of their lives under these objects, going underground only during droughts and in winter.

The red-backed salamander is named for a broad red stripe on its back, which is found on many individuals, though some are gray all over. The gray variety is known as the "leadback" morph of the species. In some areas, the leadback morph is more numerous than the red-backed morph.

SIZE: 2–4 in. long

YOUNG: The female lays 6–9 eggs, typically on the ground under logs or rocks

FOUND IN: Under debris, such as logs and rocks in deciduous forests

EBONY JEWELWING
(Calopteryx maculata)

The ebony jewelwing is a beautiful damselfly, particularly the male, which has a stunning metallic blue-green body, contrasting dramatically with his black wings. Adults of the species, like many damselflies and dragonflies, are very short-lived, surviving only for around three weeks.

Damselflies are very similar to dragonflies, but are two key differences that can help you tell them apart: First, damselflies are thinner than dragonflies. Second, when resting on plants, damselflies fold their wings behind their back, whereas dragonflies spread their wings out to the sides.

SIZE: 1.5–2.25 in. long; 1.5–2.25 in. wingspan

EGGS: The female lays about 600 eggs in slow-moving streams and rivers

FOUND IN: Areas near wooded streams and rivers

MINNESOTA

Much of northern Minnesota is a mix of forests and wetlands, but the southern part of the state is dominated by farmlands and prairie. The common nickname for Minnesota, which is the "land of 10,000 lakes," is an indication of truly how many lakes there are in the state. Because of the spatial pattern of habitats in Minnesota, much of the animal and plant diversity is found in the northern portions of the state.

RED PINE
(Pinus resinosa)

Red pine trees grow very fast and straight. They are widely planted and harvested for utility poles, fence posts, cabin logs, and lumber. They are also often grown for windbreaks, and their pretty red bark makes them popular for planting in parks.

In wild settings, red pines typically grow after intense forest fires come through, as the fire kills competing trees and shrubs, and burns the leaf litter on the ground, which kills insect pests that harm red pines.

HEIGHT: 60–80 ft.

SEASON: Cones fall in spring and summer

FOUND IN: Areas with dry, sandy or rocky soils

PINK LADY'S SLIPPER
(Cypripedium acaule)

The pink lady's slipper is a wild orchid. When in bloom it has a very showy and bulbous pink flower, which lures in bee pollinators through a narrow slit. Once inside, the only way a bee can get out is through one of two small exit holes. This is by design, so that the bee rubs against the flower's stigma on the way out. The stigma picks up pollen from the bee, which fertilizes the flower.

HEIGHT: 6–15 in.

SEASON: Flowers from late spring to early summer

FOUND IN: A wide variety of settings in shaded areas with acidic soil

RIVERBANK GRAPE
(Vitis riparia)

Riverbank grape is a vine that gets its name from where it is found—along the banks of rivers. A wide variety of animals eat its fruits, which ripen during the summer. Some birds, like gray catbirds and northern cardinals, use strips of its bark in their nests.

Riverbank grape is super hardy when it comes to cold temperatures. Its vines can survive long exposure to temperatures well below freezing. As a result, it is sometimes called the "frost grape."

HEIGHT: Up to 75 ft. long

SEASON: Flowers from late spring to early summer; fruits ripen throughout the summer

FOUND IN: A wide range of settings with moist soils and often partial shade

COMMON JEWELWEED
(Impatiens capensis)

Common jewelweed, also known as "spotted touch-me-not," often grows in dense colonies. As a result, when its bright-orange flowers are in bloom, this can result in a sea of orange color.

Common jewelweed has a long history of traditional medicinal use, dating back thousands of years. A well-known use is applying the stem and leaf sap to the skin. This can reduce pain and irritation from poison ivy, hives, and other skin ailments.

HEIGHT: 2.5–5 ft.

SEASON: Flowers from mid-summer through late fall

FOUND IN: Shady, moist areas including margins of wetlands

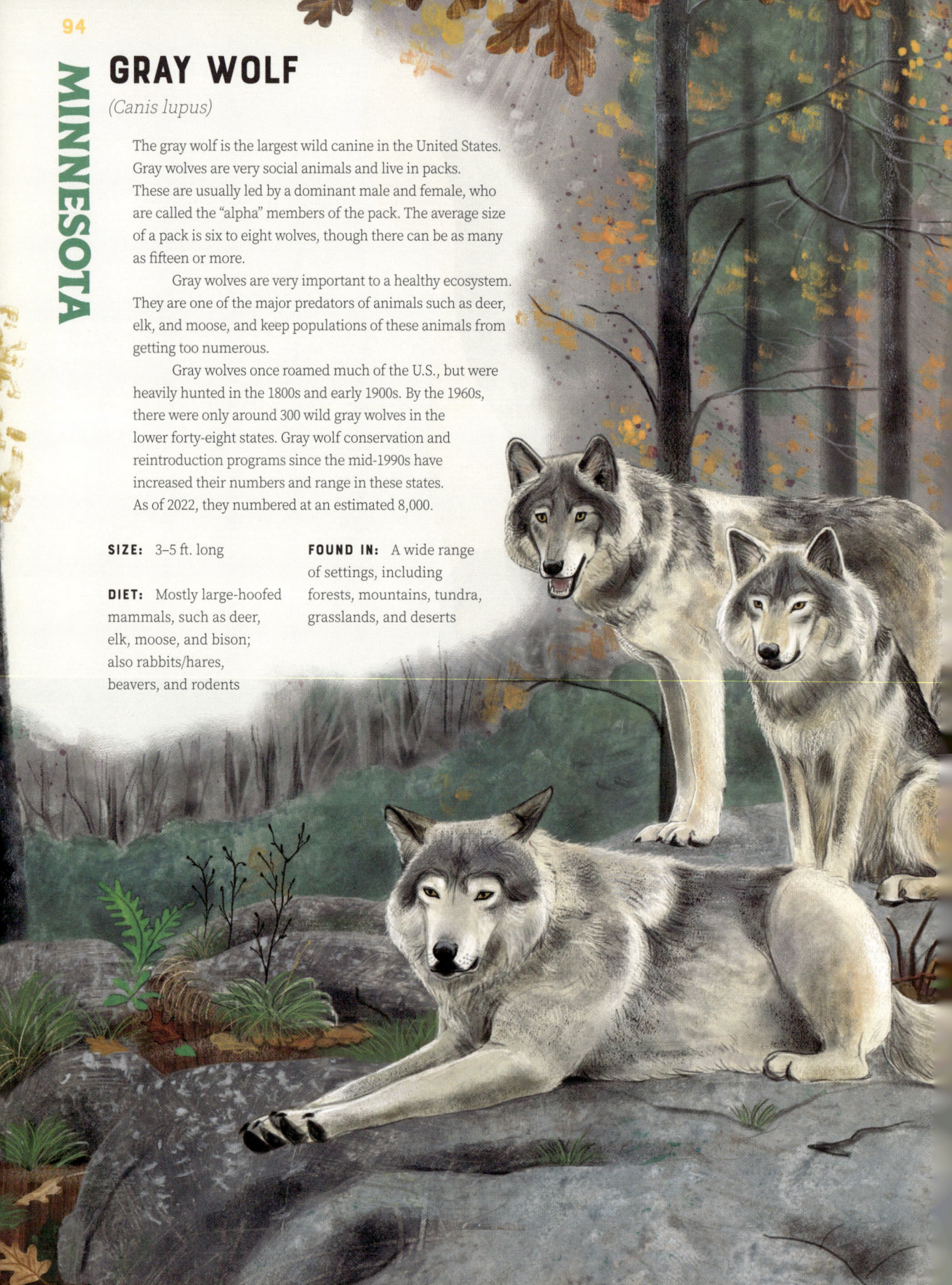

MINNESOTA

GRAY WOLF
(Canis lupus)

The gray wolf is the largest wild canine in the United States. Gray wolves are very social animals and live in packs. These are usually led by a dominant male and female, who are called the "alpha" members of the pack. The average size of a pack is six to eight wolves, though there can be as many as fifteen or more.

Gray wolves are very important to a healthy ecosystem. They are one of the major predators of animals such as deer, elk, and moose, and keep populations of these animals from getting too numerous.

Gray wolves once roamed much of the U.S., but were heavily hunted in the 1800s and early 1900s. By the 1960s, there were only around 300 wild gray wolves in the lower forty-eight states. Gray wolf conservation and reintroduction programs since the mid-1990s have increased their numbers and range in these states. As of 2022, they numbered at an estimated 8,000.

SIZE: 3–5 ft. long

DIET: Mostly large-hoofed mammals, such as deer, elk, moose, and bison; also rabbits/hares, beavers, and rodents

FOUND IN: A wide range of settings, including forests, mountains, tundra, grasslands, and deserts

COMMON LOON
(Gavia immer)

The common loon is a large duck-like waterbird. It is well known to people that live near the large bodies of water where they breed, thanks to its loud, but eerily beautiful, nighttime breeding call.

Common loons spend almost their entire life in, or on, water. They are expert divers, diving to catch fish to eat. They can dive as deep as 200 feet, and can stay underwater for five minutes.

SIZE: 2.5 ft. long; 4 ft. wingspan

DIET: Mostly fish and some aquatic invertebrates

FOUND IN: Lakes and large ponds surrounded by forest; also salt water in winter

BLACK AND GOLD BUMBLEBEE
(Bombus auricomus)

Like most bumblebee species, black and gold bumblebees live in colonies, each made up of a single queen and a large number of workers and males. The main job of the queen is to start the colony in the spring, after coming out of winter hibernation. She will then spend most of her time producing eggs throughout the summer. The workers collect food for the young, help raise them, and protect the nest. In late summer and early fall, the males and a few young females leave the nest and mate with individuals from nearby colonies. This ensures the cycle continues each year.

SIZE: 0.75–1 in. long (queens); 0.3–0.5 in. long (workers and males)

FOUND IN: A very wide variety of open settings

EGGS: The queen lays eggs all summer

Mississippi

Much like Louisiana to its west, Mississippi is a very flat state. Its highest elevation is only 807 feet above sea level! About sixty percent of the state is forested, and thirty percent is agricultural land, with the rest being a mix of land types. Mississippi and Louisiana have very similar animal and plant communities given their geographic proximity, the habitat types they share, and their similar overall size.

SOUTHERN MAGNOLIA
(Magnolia grandiflora)

The southern magnolia is the state tree of Mississippi. It is a broadleaf evergreen tree, which is an uncommon combination. It is well known for its large, beautiful flowers, which are around eight inches across and mostly bloom in the spring.

Southern magnolias are very popular ornamental trees. People often plant them in their yards in suburban areas. They are one of the most wind-resistant trees in the southern U.S. As a result, they are a popular choice for planting in parks in hurricane-prone areas.

HEIGHT: 60–80 ft.

SEASON: Flowers mostly in spring, though additional flowers also appear in summer and fall

FOUND IN: Areas of moist soils, often along streams and rivers and nearby swamps

YAUPON HOLLY
(Ilex vomitoria)

Yaupon holly, like southern magnolia, has the uncommon combination of being both a broadleaf and an evergreen plant. It is often grown in a hedge-like manner in people's yards. Because its branches and leaves grow so densely, some people trim the shrubs into specific shapes and designs. They produce lots of small fruits that remain on the plant through winter and into the spring. They're eaten by many different birds, making yaupon holly great for wildlife-friendly yards.

HEIGHT: 10–20 ft.

SEASON: Flowers bloom in spring; fruits ripen from late fall and last into spring

FOUND IN: A wide range of settings, most frequently areas with sandy soils

LANCE-LEAVED COREOPSIS
(Coreopsis lanceolata)

Lance-leaved coreopsis, along with other species of coreopsis, are also sometimes called "tickseed" because their seeds look like ticks. This plant is a very popular choice for wildflower gardens thanks to its beautiful tall, yellow flowers. These attract many pollinators, like bees and butterflies, and are very hardy in various soils and environments. Once seeded, these plants often don't need watering, even during extreme droughts.

HEIGHT: 1.5–3 ft.

SEASON: Flowers bloom from late spring well into fall

FOUND IN: Almost any non-wetland, open setting with lots of sun exposure

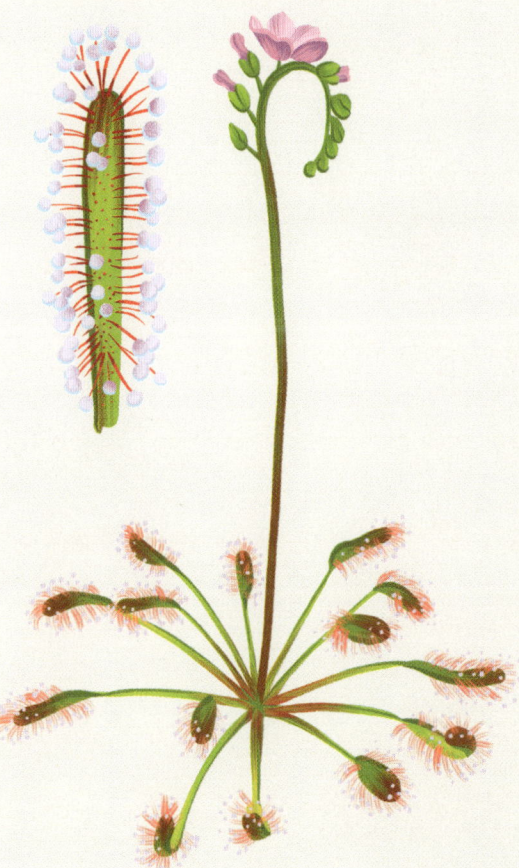

PINK SUNDEW
(Drosera capillaris)

Pink sundew is an insect-eating wildflower that grows in wet and damp places. Its name comes from the drops of liquid at the tips of the tentacle-like hairs on its leaves. This liquid is a sticky secretion that helps the flower capture any small insects that land on it. It is very acidic, which helps with digesting the captured insects. When an insect is captured, the leaf folds in on itself, stopping the insect from escaping.

HEIGHT: 1–2 in.

SEASON: Flowers blooms primarily in spring, but sometimes in summer or fall

FOUND IN: Areas with wet acidic soils, such as bogs and pine savannas

Mississippi

SWAMP RABBIT
(Sylvilagus aquaticus)

The swamp rabbit is the largest cottontail rabbit in the U.S., named for its habitat—in, and near, freshwater wetlands. Skilled swimmers, these rabbits will jump in the water and swim away if a predator threatens them. They eat a lot of different aquatic plants, often while in the water. Their thick fur helps to waterproof their skin.

Swamp rabbits are most active during the late evening and at night. During the daytime, they hide under cover of dense thickets of shrubs or inside fallen trees.

SIZE: 18–22 in. long

DIET: Grasses, sedges, aquatic plants, leaves, bark, fruit, and more

FOUND IN: Along edges and shallow areas of a wide range of freshwater wetland types

GREAT EGRET
(Ardea alba)

The great egret is a tall, white wading bird that is often seen hunting in marshes. These birds are very stealthy when hunting, often standing still in a shallow area of water as they wait for their prey to come into range. They will then strike very quickly with their long bills.

Great egrets nest in colonies, often with other types of egrets as well as herons. Pairs will each tend to their large nest, up in a tree. This will often be found in, or along the edge of, a wetland, and can be as high as 100 feet above the ground.

SIZE: 3 ft. long; 4 ft. wingspan

DIET: Mostly fish, amphibians, and crayfish

FOUND IN: A wide range of freshwater and saltwater wetlands/marshes

GREEN TREE FROG
(Hyla cinerea)

Like most other tree frogs, green tree frogs have "toe pads," which are round, adhesive disks. These help them climb almost any surface, even perfectly vertical ones, including trees, shrubs, and the sides of houses.

Like other amphibians, green tree frogs are at risk of drying out. They have an interesting adaptation to help avoid this: When it gets very dry, they sometimes use their feet to wipe a mucous-like secretion over their bodies, helping to reduce water loss.

SIZE: 1.25–2.25 in. long

EGGS: The female lays around 400 eggs, attached underwater to aquatic vegetation

FOUND IN: A wide range of freshwater wetlands containing abundant aquatic vegetation

SPICEBUSH SWALLOWTAIL
(Papilio troilus)

The spicebush swallowtail gets its name from where it lays its eggs—on spicebush plants, since its caterpillars like to eat spicebush leaves. It will also lay eggs on other related plants, however, such as sassafras, ash, and tulip trees.

Swallowtail butterflies are often seen at mud puddles, where it looks like they are drinking the water. In reality, they are extracting salt and other minerals to help them reproduce. This is a behavior known as "puddling," and some other butterfly species do this too.

SIZE: 2 in. long; 3.5–4.5 in. wingspan

EGGS: The female lays her eggs on the underside of leaves of host plants

FOUND IN: Deciduous woodlands, fields, gardens, and the edges of streams and rivers

MISSOURI

Even though Missouri is only the thirtieth-largest state in the U.S., most of which (about sixty-five percent) is covered by agricultural land, it has a relatively high species diversity. This is largely due to the wide range of habitats found in the state, ranging from grasslands and prairies to the extensive floodplains of the Mississippi and Missouri Rivers, and the rugged Ozark Mountains.

FLOWERING DOGWOOD
(Cornus florida)

Flowering dogwood is the state tree of Missouri. When in bloom in early spring, the entire crown of the tree is covered in beautiful, big white flowers, and in the fall the leaves turn a stunning scarlet red. These attributes make it a very popular tree to plant in yards.

Indigenous communities have historically made a remedy for malaria from the bark and roots of flowering dogwood. They also made red dye from the roots, which people continue to do today. The wood is very dense and hard, and is used to make a wide range of items including wooden mallets, tool handles, cutting boards, and much more.

HEIGHT: 20–40 ft.

SEASON: Flowers in early spring; fruits ripen in early fall

FOUND IN: A wide variety of settings, most frequently in shaded areas under larger trees

AMERICAN PERSIMMON
(Diospyros virginiana)

The American persimmon is a medium-sized tree that is best known for its fruits. These are high in vitamin C, and eaten by humans, along with a wide range of birds and other mammals. The ripe fruit can be eaten raw, and the pulp is often made into jelly, pies, puddings, and even candy. Some people even dry and roast the seeds to use as a substitute for coffee. In some places, the nectar from American persimmon flowers are important for honey production.

HEIGHT: 30–80 ft.

SEASON: Flowers in late spring; fruits ripen between early fall and early winter

FOUND IN: An extremely wide range of settings, most commonly along woodland edges

BUTTERWEED
(Packera glabella)

Despite its alluring name, which comes from the butter-yellow color of its flowers, butterweed is toxic to humans, horses, and cattle if eaten.

Butterweed is a winter annual. The leaves at the base of the plant emerge in the fall and the plant continues to grow throughout the winter. It is often one of the few herbaceous plants that grow in winter in many of its locations. With this head start, it can bloom first in early spring.

HEIGHT: 1–3 ft.

SEASON: Flowers bloom in very early spring

FOUND IN: Damp areas in woodlands and along the edges of streams, rivers, and other wetlands

VIOLET WOOD-SORREL
(Oxalis violacea)

Violet wood-sorrel produces small and beautiful violet-colored flowers. All parts of the plant, including these flowers, are edible to humans, but only in modest amounts. Many indigenous communities have harvested violet wood-sorrel for food. Today, the flowers are often added to salads. They are a sour, but edible, ornamental ingredient.

HEIGHT: 4–8 in.

SEASON: Blooms twice per year, in late spring and early fall

FOUND IN: Open woodlands and a wide variety of open settings, usually in areas with acidic soils

MISSOURI

GRAY FOX
(*Urocyon cinereoargenteus*)

The gray fox, though common and widespread, is rarely seen by people. This is mainly because these foxes are nocturnal and spend a lot of time in trees. Gray foxes are the only canines in the U.S. that readily climb trees, which they can do thanks to their semi-retractable claws. Spending time up in trees helps keep gray foxes safe from predators such as coyotes. It also gives them access to more food, like birds, birds' eggs, and flying squirrels.

SIZE: 20–30 in. long

DIET: Small mammals, birds, amphibians, reptiles, nuts, and fruits

FOUND IN: Dense deciduous forests, thickets, and swamps

EASTERN BLUEBIRD
(*Sialia sialis*)

Eastern bluebirds nest in tree cavities—often cavities made by woodpeckers in previous years. The male brings nesting material to a potential nesting cavity, where he tries to attract a female, perching above or nearby and flapping his wings to get her attention.

A pair of eastern bluebirds will often raise two sets of young ("broods") in a year. Sometimes young from the first brood will help raise the second brood. Young from the second brood of the year may remain with their parents for the winter.

SIZE: 7 in. long; 1 ft. wingspan

DIET: Insects, fruits, and berries

FOUND IN: Open woodlands, forest clearings, beaver wetlands, meadows, and orchards

RED-EARED SLIDER
(Trachemys scripta elegans)

Red-eared sliders live in a wide variety of wetland types and can even tolerate brackish water. They are often seen by people, as they like to bask in the sun, sometimes on exposed logs and rocks.

Red-eared sliders are one of the most sold turtles in the pet trade. Unfortunately, many pet red-eared sliders are released into the wild by their owners, which can harm natural environments by introducing parasites and diseases. It can also cause declines in native turtle species outcompeted by red-eared sliders.

SIZE: 5–11 in. long

EGGS: The female lays 6–12 eggs in an underground nest that she digs herself

FOUND IN: A wide variety of freshwater wetlands, especially those with muddy bottoms and a lot of aquatic vegetation

LIGATED FURROW BEE
(Halictus ligatus)

The ligated furrow bee is one of over 4,000 native U.S. bees. Furrow bees are often called "sweat bees," as they are attracted to sweat produced by humans. This is because they need a lot of sodium in their diet, which is very concentrated in sweat. The bees' tongues have even evolved to a shape that optimizes their ability to lick sweat from human skin. But don't worry, they will only sting you if you harass them. And their stingers are so small that their sting is not very painful.

SIZE: 0.3–0.4 in.

EGGS: The female lays a single egg in each of a number of underground tunnels, and leaves a store of pollen (for food) before sealing off each one

FOUND IN: A wide variety of settings, particularly sandy areas

Montana

Montana is a large state—the fourth-largest in the U.S. Much of it is remote and undeveloped. The state has many kinds of ecosystems, from mountains and forests to grasslands and river valleys.

PONDEROSA PINE
(Pinus ponderosa)

The ponderosa pine is one of the most widespread trees in the western U.S. Many know it for its striking orange bark, which is described as smelling like either butterscotch or vanilla. This bark gives off the most smell when it's in direct sunlight.

Ponderosa pine bark is very thick, often upwards of 6 inches. This helps the tree survive the frequent, low-intensity fires in many ponderosa pine forests. These fires are important for ponderosa pines, as they stop competing trees from taking over. The fires also help ponderosa pine cones to open and release their seeds.

HEIGHT: 60–120 ft.

FOUND IN: Dry mountain slopes

SEASON: Flowers in late spring, seeds drop in early fall

FAIRY SLIPPER
(Calypso bulbosa)

The fairy slipper is a lovely little orchid. It blooms on the forest floor of conifer forests. Though widespread, it is quite rare in most of the areas where it exists.

The fairy slipper relies heavily on pollination by newly emerged queen bumblebees. It tricks pollinators into thinking its bright, sweet-smelling flowers will provide nectar. However, unlike most orchids, it doesn't provide its pollinators with any such reward. As a result, these insect pollinators soon learn not to revisit its flowers.

HEIGHT: 3–9 in.

SEASON: Flowers from mid-spring to early summer

FOUND IN: Cool, damp, shady coniferous woodlands—even in bogs and white cedar swamps

BITTERROOT
(Lewisia rediviva)

The bitterroot is the state flower of Montana. It is a small herbaceous plant, often found in quite dry areas. Though it is a small plant, it has a disproportionately large flower that is quite beautiful. Its flower can be anywhere from white to a deep pink, or a combination of these.

There is a long history of different indigenous communities eating parts of this plant in a variety of ways. As the name suggests, its roots are quite bitter, so it's often mixed with berries or meat.

HEIGHT: 2–3 in.

FOUND IN: Dry areas with gravelly or sandy soils

SEASON: Flowers from mid-spring to mid-summer

THIMBLEBERRY
(Rubus parviflorus)

The thimbleberry got its name because its fruits resemble a thimble. Thimbleberries are red and similar to raspberries, but smaller and a bit more sour. They are popular among many types of animals, as well as with people. People eat these berries raw or cook them and make them into a jelly. The shoots that grow in the spring can be eaten like a vegetable, and some people make soap from the stems of the plant.

HEIGHT: 3–8 ft.

SEASON: Flowers from late spring to mid-summer

FOUND IN: Shrublands, openings in and edges of forests/woodlands, and along rivers

Montana

BLACK-BILLED MAGPIE
(Pica hudsonia)

Black-billed magpies construct impressive nests. A male and female pair will work together to build a tall, dome-shaped nest about 3 by 4 feet in size. These nests are fully enclosed, with a single opening on one side, and are made of sticks, mud, and sometimes animal hair, often from horses. They take upwards of thirty days to build.

Black-billed magpies live on invertebrates they find on the ground, as well as ticks from the backs of large animals like elk, bison, and cattle. They also follow around large predators (such as wolves) and scavenge from what they kill.

SIZE: 1.5–2 ft. long; 2 ft. wingspan

DIET: Mostly insects, but also amphibians and reptiles, birds and eggs, small mammals, carrion, seeds, and fruit

FOUND IN: Open areas (that have some trees and/or shrubs) and near water

WESTERN TOAD
(Anaxyrus boreas)

The western toad, or the "boreal toad," is active mainly during warm times of the day, at least during the spring and fall. During the hot summer months, they are active mainly at night, so that they don't overheat and/or become dehydrated.

Western toads have toxins that help keep them safe from many predators. This is particularly important because they move rather slowly. They walk and hop, but can't jump, which limits their ability to escape from many predators.

SIZE: 3–5 in. long

FOUND IN: Open areas near freshwater

EGGS: The female lays paired, spaghetti-like strings containing 3,000–15,000 eggs

GRIZZLY BEAR
(Ursus arctos horribilis)

The grizzly bear, often referred to as a "grizzly," is a subspecies of the brown bear. You can identify them both by their dark color, but also their large size—they're often tall, with a large shoulder hump. This hump, which you don't see on the black bear, is formed by the group of muscles that gives grizzy bears the strength they need for digging. This, and the long and sharp claws on their front feet, helps them dig for food (mostly vegetation) and make their dens.

Currently there are only about 2,000 wild grizzly bears in the lower forty-eight states. It is estimated that there may have once been around 50,000 in that area, but over time they have declined, primarily as a result of historic hunting, because people are so afraid of them. They are currently protected under the federal Endangered Species Act and, fortunately, their numbers are increasing, though quite slowly. They'll likely never reach their former numbers due to loss of habitat.

SIZE: 3.5 ft. tall to the shoulder; 6–7 ft. long

DIET: Vegetation such as roots, berries, grass, and forbs. Also fish, ground squirrels, hoofed animals (deer, caribou, etc.), and carrion

FOUND IN: Forests, alpine meadows, and areas along rivers, varying in location across the year

NEBRASKA

For its moderately large size, Nebraska doesn't have that much habitat diversity. Most of the state is grasslands, prairies, and farmland. Rolling hills, called "sandhills," cover much of north-central Nebraska. As you move from east to west, the elevation gradually increases, ranging from 800 to 5,400 feet.

HONEY LOCUST
(Gleditsia triacanthos)

The honey locust got part of its name from its large seed pods. The pulp in these tastes somewhat like honey. Honey locust trees are covered in large thorns that can sometimes exceed 6 inches long. These thorns protect the tree from large herbivores. In the past, this included mastodons!

The honey locust is a very hardy tree. It can tolerate salt spray, polluted soils, drought, and other harsh conditions. As a result, it is often planted in urban areas, where many other trees are unable to survive.

HEIGHT: 60–100 ft.

SEASON: Flowers mid- to late spring; fruits from early fall to mid-winter

FOUND IN: A wide range of settings, as long they get abundant sun

HOARY VERVAIN
(Verbena stricta)

Hoary vervain, also often called "hoary verbena," is like a pollinator magnet. Each of its (up to three) flowering stalks produces many lavender-colored flowers, which bloom for four to six weeks in the summer. The first flowers to open on each stalk are those at the bottom, and the ones above follow. Many bees, flies, butterflies, and even ants feed on their nectar, as do ruby-throated hummingbirds. This is the only plant that the caterpillars of the common buckeye butterfly will feed on.

HEIGHT: 2–4 ft.

SEASON: Flowers throughout much of summer

FOUND IN: Sunny, dry, open areas

CHOKECHERRY
(Prunus virginiana)

The chokecherry is a very important source of food for a lot of animals. Many birds and mammals gorge themselves on the fruits. Herbivores like elk, deer, moose, and rabbits eat the plant's leaves, twigs, and buds. Its abundant spring flowers provide nectar for many pollinators.

Many indigenous communities have made use of the chokecherry's fruits for a variety of foods. The bark and roots can be made into a mixture believed to fight colds and stomach issues. Its wood is also burned in some ceremonial rituals.

HEIGHT: 20–30 ft.

SEASON: Flowers mid-spring to early summer; fruits ripen in late summer

FOUND IN: A wide range of settings, as long as they get some sunshine and soils aren't too wet

THISTLE POPPY
(Argemone polyanthemos)

The thistle poppy is also called "prickly poppy," as its stems and leaf edges are covered in prickles. Grazing animals, like cows, know not to eat them, so they tend to grow in relatively large numbers in areas grazed by cows. The seeds are toxic to mammals. But some birds, like turkeys, quails, and doves, can eat them without harm.

HEIGHT: 2–3 ft.

SEASON: Flowers late spring and throughout summer

FOUND IN: Dry, open settings

NEBRASKA

BLACK-TAILED PRAIRIE DOG
(Cynomys ludovicianus)

Black-tailed prairie dogs live in large colonies called "towns" or "villages." These are extensive underground burrow systems. Living together in large colonies helps protect the species against predators—more pairs of eyes to watch out for each other.

Black-tailed prairie dogs are very important to the healthy functioning of their ecosystem. They are a key food source for the critically endangered black-footed ferret. They also are an important food for larger predators like hawks, eagles, coyotes, and foxes. Many animals use vacant prairie dog burrows. They include rabbits, burrowing owls, rattlesnakes, foxes, and rodents.

SIZE: 1–1.5 ft. long

FOUND IN: Flat, dry, sparsely vegetated grasslands

DIET: Mostly grasses and leafy vegetation; some insects, occasionally

MOURNING DOVE
(Zenaida macroura)

The mourning dove is one of the most populous birds in the U.S. They are avid seed eaters, often eating thousands of grass seeds per day. They intentionally eat bits of sand and gravel to help digest these seeds.

Mourning doves have a unique way of helping their young: Both the male and female produce a milk-like liquid, which they store in a part of their throat. They feed it to their young during their first one to two weeks of life. This liquid is full of nutrients. It helps boost the chicks' immune systems.

SIZE: 1 ft. long; 1.5 ft. wingspan

FOUND IN: A wide variety of open to partially open areas

DIET: Seeds and grains

AMERICAN BULLFROG
(Lithobates catesbeianus)

The American bullfrog is the largest frog in the U.S. It is so big that it eats other frogs, rodents, small snakes, and sometimes birds.

Bullfrogs are most often found in, and on the edges of, large wetlands like ponds and lakes. The male will take a territory along the shoreline, calling "jug-o-rum" to attract a mate. If another male enters his territory, he will defend it, lunging at the intruder and sometimes wrestling with him.

SIZE: 4–8 in. long

EGGS: The female lays 10,000–20,000 eggs in a large mat

FOUND IN: Freshwater wetlands such as lakes, ponds, marshes, and rivers

RED MILKWEED BEETLE
(Tetraopes tetrophthalmus)

This beetle relies an enormous amount on common milkweed, which it uses it for food, to lay eggs, and for protection. After red milkweed beetle larvae hatch from their eggs in the fall, they start digging underground, feeding on the roots of the milkweed. Then they burrow into the milkweed's roots and overwinter inside them. Like monarch butterfly caterpillars, red milkweed beetles gain protection from predators by feeding on milkweed, since they incorporate its toxins into their bodies.

SIZE: 0.5 in. long

EGGS: The female lays groups of 30 eggs; she can lay up to as many as 2,000 over her one-month adult lifespan

FOUND IN: Areas where you would find host milkweed plants, which tend to be sunny, open areas

Nevada

Nevada is a vast state, much of which is largely undeveloped. It has diverse ecosystems, from deserts to forests and mountains. Much of the state is dry, so many animals and plants there have adapted to arid environments.

GREAT BASIN BRISTLECONE PINE
(Pinus longaeva)

The Great Basin bristlecone pine is one of the oldest trees in the world. One was aged at 5,065 years, and another at 4,847. This means that they were alive even before the Great Pyramids of Egypt were built. It is likely that there are even older ones that haven't yet been aged. Scientists keep their locations secret to protect them because visitors may cause harm, either intentionally or accidentally.

Great Basin bristlecone pines live in extremely harsh environments—high, rocky, nutrient-poor ridges. Winter temperatures regularly drop below freezing, and the winds can be extreme. This makes the pines grow in twisted shapes. Even in these conditions, they survive for an incredibly long time.

HEIGHT: 40–60 ft.

SEASON: Pollen is shed in mid-summer; cones open in early fall

FOUND IN: High-elevation, dry, rocky settings

SINGLE-LEAF PINYON
(Pinus monophylla)

The single-leaf pinyon, or "pinyon pine," is widespread in the high deserts of the southwestern U.S. It most often grows with junipers in pinyon-juniper woodlands.

Single-leaf pinyon is the only single-needle pine species in the world. It is best known for the seeds from its cones, which are harvested, roasted, and sold as "pine nuts." Many wildlife species feed on these seeds. The pinyon jay is a particularly important one. This jay harvests many seeds and hides some of them underground to come back and eat later. Many of these are never revisited by the jay, and therefore they grow into new trees.

HEIGHT: 20–40 ft.

SEASON: Pollen is shed in late spring/early summer; cones open in late summer

FOUND IN: Dry, rocky mountain slopes and ridges, typically 3,000–9,000 feet in elevation

SAGEBRUSH
(Artemisia tridentata)

The sagebrush, though a somewhat short shrub, is an incredibly important one. Its root systems help keep the soil in place, and help to reduce erosion. This is crucial in areas recently disturbed by oil and gas mining. They also act as a "nurse plant" for other plant species, which they do by providing shade and moisture. This helps many grasses and forbs to grow successfully. Many animals, including the greater sage-grouse, rely on them for food and habitat.

HEIGHT: 4–12 ft.

SEASON: Flowers bloom mid- to late summer (sometimes later depending on the location)

FOUND IN: Dry flats/plains, rolling hills, and rocky slopes

BIGHORN SHEEP
(Ovis canadensis)

Bighorn sheep spend much of their life in steep, rocky, mountainous terrain. They are very skilled climbers, as their hooves are well designed for this type of ground. They live in these extreme environments to avoid predators, like bears, mountain lions, and coyotes. Bighorn sheep have very sharp eyesight, which is the main sense they use to detect predators. The open, mostly barren high mountains let them see for a long way. This reduces their risk of being ambushed by predators. Both the males and females have horns, though the males' are much larger and more curved that the females'.

SIZE: 2.5–3 ft. tall, 5 ft. long (females); 3 ft. tall, 6 ft. long (males)

FOUND IN: High elevation areas, rocky slopes, and alpine grasslands

DIET: Grasses, woody plants, and cacti

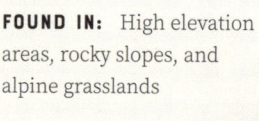

GREATER SAGE-GROUSE
(Centrocercus urophasianus)

The greater sage-grouse is one of the iconic species of the sagebrush ecosystem. Most people know them for their amazing courtship displays, which groups of males perform to attract females. Each male puffs up his chest, causing him to turn almost circular in shape. Two large yellow air sacs on his chest inflate, contrasting with his bright-white chest feathers. He spreads out his tail feathers into a semi-circle shape, made of some twenty large feather spikes, and starts to strut his stuff. His "dance" involves series of dramatic head thrusts and a mix of vocalizations. These include coos, pops, whistles, and even a huff.

SIZE: 1.5–2 ft. long (females); 2–2.5 ft. long (males); 2.5 ft. wingspan

FOUND IN: Sagebrush plains

DIET: Most parts of green plants as well seeds and insects

DESERT TORTOISE
(Gopherus agassizii)

Desert tortoises are well adapted to the harsh deserts where they live. They are able to store water in their bladders for long stretches of time, so they don't need regular access to water. They have long, sharp claws that help them effectively walk in sand, as well as to dig burrows. These underground burrows let them stay warm in winter and escape the summer heat. They also dig depressions in the sand as a way to concentrate rainwater.

SIZE: 9–15 in. long

EGGS: The female lays 2–12 eggs in an underground nest she digs herself

FOUND IN: Dry, sandy, and rocky sparsely vegetated settings

VIVID DANCER DAMSELFLY
(Argia vivida)

The vivid dancer damselfly is Nevada's state insect. They are one of the most stunningly beautiful of all damselflies in the U.S., the males in particular. Males are mostly a very bright blue, including their eyes, but they have black bands and patches on their bodies and tails. Vivid dancer damselflies live in forests, where they seek sunny spots to bask in and warm up. At night, they settle on trees, which helps reduce the amount of heat loss from their bodies.

SIZE: 1–1.5 in. long

EGGS: The female lays eggs on vegetation just under the water's surface

FOUND IN: Springs, seeps, and streams in forested areas

NEW HAMPSHIRE

New Hampshire is the fifth-smallest state. It is mostly forested, with a wide variety of forest types. Lower-elevation forests make up much of the southern part of the state, and mountains dominate the northern part. This is where the infamous Mount Washington is located. One of the highest wind speeds ever recorded (231 miles per hour) took place at its summit.

AMERICAN WHITE BIRCH
(Betula papyrifera)

The American white birch has bark that peels away from the tree as it grows wider, and is sometimes called "paper birch" as a result. When it sheds its older bark, it leaves new bark underneath, like how a snake sheds its skin as it grows.

This tree also has the nickname "canoe birch," as indigenous communities historically made canoes from its wood. Today, many interesting products are made from this tree. The sap is used to make non-alcoholic birch beer, syrup, and vinegar. The wood is used to make toothpicks, ice cream sticks, clothespins, broom handles, and much more.

HEIGHT: 50–70 ft.

SEASON: Flowers mid- to late spring

FOUND IN: Cool, moist areas in existing forests or woodlands

RED-BERRIED ELDER
(Sambucus racemosa)

Red-berried elder, also known as the "red elderberry," is a member of the honeysuckle family. As with other plants in that family, its flowers are quite fragrant. They attract a lot of pollinators when they are in flower early in the springtime. But their leaves, when crushed, smell notably foul. This is an adaptation to keep them from being eaten by certain animals.

The bright-red berries of this plant are toxic to humans if eaten raw, but birds have no problem eating them, and feed away heavily. For that reason, many people plant these in their yards to provide a natural food source for birds.

HEIGHT: 6–14 ft.

SEASON: Flowers early spring; fruits mid-summer

FOUND IN: Mature hardwood forests and sometimes along the edges of streams and rivers

CANADA BUNCHBERRY
(Cornus canadensis)

The Canada bunchberry is also often called "creeping dogwood." It is a dogwood, though unlike other dogwoods, it doesn't grow as a tree. Canada bunchberry grows as a creeping mat of vegetation instead.

Like many plants, the Canada bunchberry is pollinated by insects. The way this happens is a feat of nature: When a pollinator touches the flower's center, its stamens launch pollen in under half a millisecond, meaning if it did this for a whole second, it would happen 2,000 times! In fact, this is one of the fastest-recorded plant movements in the world.

HEIGHT: 4–8 in.

SEASON: Flowers late spring to mid-summer; fruits present mid-summer to mid fall

FOUND IN: A variety of moist habitats including forests, bogs, and wet meadows

PURPLE PITCHER PLANT
(Sarracenia purpurea)

This plant is called a "pitcher plant" because it is shaped somewhat like a pitcher of water. Rainwater collects in the "pitcher," which fills right up, attracting various invertebrates. Many of these can't escape from the water and drown. Mosquito larvae, the larvae of other flies, and other decomposers feed on these drowned invertebrates, or they are decomposed by bacteria in the water. The pitcher plant then absorbs nutrients in the waste released by decomposers. The purple pitcher plant is therefore carnivorous, but because of this indirect process, it doesn't need to make digestive enzymes like many other carnivorous plants.

HEIGHT: 1–2 ft.

SEASON: Flowers from mid-spring through summer

FOUND IN: Bogs, fens, marshes, roadside ditches, and wet coniferous forest floors

NEW HAMPSHIRE

MOOSE
(Alces alces)

The moose is the largest member of the deer family. To grow to this size, and maintain it, they have to eat 40–60 pounds of plants every day. At its birth in the spring, a newborn moose (a "calf") weighs 20–25 pounds. By the fall, they have already reached 300–400 pounds!

Male moose ("bulls") grow notably larger than females ("cows"). Bulls also grow antlers each year. Their antlers can grow to be up to 5 feet wide and weigh up to 50 pounds. In the mating season, they serve as the sign of a bull's strength, and are used in male-to-male fights over females.

SIZE: 6 ft. tall at the shoulders, 8–10 ft. long

FOUND IN: Forests interspersed with wetlands

DIET: Plant material, including soft, green vegetation in summer; twigs, buds, bark, and conifer needles in winter

BLACK-CAPPED CHICKADEE
(Poecile atricapillus)

Black-capped chickadees are common and frequent visitors to backyard bird feeders. This is true across their range. They seemingly have an endless appetite, continually returning for seeds. In reality, they store the seeds that they take in some other location to eat later.

The black-capped chickadee got its name from its call, which sounds like "chick-a-dee-dee-dee." It uses this call sometimes to communicate to others that a predator is nearby. The greater the need for warning, the more "dee" notes it will add to the end.

SIZE: 5 in. long; 8 in. wingspan

FOUND IN: Forests, open woodlands, and suburban areas with trees and shrubs

DIET: Mostly insects during spring and fall; a mix of insects, seeds, and berries in winter

SPOTTED SALAMANDER
(Ambystoma maculatum)

A spotted salamander is truly a sight to see, and one that will put a smile on the face of most anyone. Each one has a unique pattern of spots and what looks like a permanent smile on its face.

Though fairly common where they exist, spotted salamanders are rarely seen by people. They spend the great majority of their lives underground, in small mammal burrows. People only see them during breeding migrations on warm, rainy, early spring nights.

SIZE: 5–9 in. long

EGGS: The female lays several jelly-like masses, each containing 50–100 eggs

FOUND IN: Forested areas near freshwater wetlands, such as vernal pools and swamps

EASTERN BLACK CARPENTER ANT
(Camponotus pennsylvanicus)

The eastern black carpenter ant gets its name because it makes its nests in wood, chewing its way through wood without eating it. This also helps with the natural process of decomposition.

These ants live in colonies, made up of a queen and a large number of workers. One of their favorite foods is a sugary, dew-like juice secreted by aphids. Eastern black carpenter ants will "farm" the aphids for their sweet juice, providing protection and food to the aphids in return. For this reason, some people refer to aphids as "ant-cows."

SIZE: 0.25–0.5 in. long (workers); 0.5–0.75 in. long (queens)

EGGS: The queen lays several hundred eggs, twice per year (in early spring and late summer)

FOUND IN: Forest edges, woodlands, and suburban areas

New Jersey

New Jersey is very biodiverse for its size. It is only the forty-seventh-largest state, yet ranks thirty-second in its biodiversity. Much of this is due to the wide diversity of ecotypes found in New Jersey. These include forest types (including the vast pine barrens of southern New Jersey), wetlands, and coastal environments. There is also a wide diversity of unique highland ecosystems in the northern parts of the state.

NORTHERN RED OAK
(Quercus rubra)

The northern red oak, commonly referred to as simply the "red oak," is the state tree of New Jersey. It is a relatively fast-growing tree and can live for 200–300 years. These traits, plus its adaptability, make it a popular shade tree for lawns, parks, and golf courses. These trees also attract a lot of wildlife, which use them as nesting sites and feed on their acorns.

The northern red oak is a popular tree for timber. It is often used to make flooring, furniture, and cabinets, and many people use it for firewood, too.

HEIGHT: 60–80 ft.

SEASON: Flowers in mid-spring; drops acorns throughout the fall

FOUND IN: A wide range of settings, as long as the soil is somewhat rich

SWEET PEPPERBUSH
(Clethra alnifolia)

Sweet pepperbush is a highly adaptable shrub. Its preferred habitat is in very moist soils, often in marshes, on mats of moss in bogs, and in wet woods. Yet, when planted by people in other settings, such as in sunny and dry backyards, it can do fairly well.

Sweet pepperbush was named for its very sweet-smelling flowers. It blooms in long stalks in mid-summer. These attract many bees, butterflies, and even hummingbirds. After the flowers have bloomed, many seed capsules remain on the tall stalk, looking like a bunch of peppercorns. That's where the plant gets the "pepper" part of its name.

HEIGHT: 4–8 ft.

SEASON: Flowers in mid-summer

FOUND IN: Swamps, marshes, bogs, wet thickets, and along pond and lake edges

AMERICAN WINTERGREEN
(Gaultheria procumbens)

American wintergreen is a low-growing evergreen plant. It is actually a type of shrub, even though it only grows 4–6 inches tall. It gets its name because it is a natural source of the minty wintergreen flavor in many gums, toothpastes, teas (also called "teaberry"), and other products.

Despite its minty flavor, relatively few animals feed on it. Deer, some small mammals, and some ground-feeding birds will eat it. These birds include grouse, bobwhite, and pheasants. Eastern chipmunks really like it for some reason, though for most other animals, it's off the menu.

HEIGHT: 4–6 in.

SEASON: Flowers throughout much of summer; berries present in fall through winter; leaves are kept year-round

FOUND IN: Shady woodlands and forests, particularly those with hardwood trees

COMMON BLUE VIOLET
(Viola sororia)

The common blue violet, or "purple violet," blooms early in the spring, before many other plants have started to flower. As a result, it is a vital source of nectar for many early season bees, butterflies, and other pollinators.

While they do reproduce with the help of pollinators, this plant also has other ways of doing so. It can spread using a complex, underground root system called "rhizomes." Ants also bring its seeds back to their nests, where they are covered in a nutrient-rich substance and partially digested by ant larvae. Because the seeds aren't fully digested, they are essentially planted in the larvae's waste piles.

HEIGHT: 3–6 in.

SEASON: Flowers in early to mid-spring

FOUND IN: Shady areas in woods, thickets, streambeds, and yards

New Jersey

STRIPED SKUNK
(Mephitis mephitis)

The striped skunk, more commonly just called a "skunk," is well known for its foul smell. This comes from an oily liquid that it sprays at potential predators when it feels threatened. Striped skunks can spray this liquid 10–15 feet, and its odor can be detected well over half a mile away.

Striped Skunks have long claws, sharp teeth, and a strong sense of smell. These are all adaptations to help them find food, mostly insects. They use their claws to dig into the soil and also to tear apart rotting logs and stumps to search for insects.

SIZE: 2.5 ft. long, 5–8 in. tall at the shoulder

DIET: A variety of vegetation, invertebrates, bird and turtle eggs, and carrion

FOUND IN: A wide diversity of settings ranging from woodlands, meadows, deserts, and prairies to urban and suburban areas

PINE BARRENS TREE FROG
(Dryophytes andersonii)

Many consider the Pine Barrens tree frog the most beautiful frog in the U.S. Its mostly green body helps it blend into the pine woodlands where it lives. Along each side of its body is a lavender-colored stripe, bordered in white, and the underside of its legs are bright orange. This bright orange serves as a warning to predators that the frog is toxic.

Pine Barrens tree frogs live in three separate areas: the New Jersey Pine Barrens, the Carolina Sandhills, and southern Alabama and Florida's panhandle. This is especially different from the continuous distributions of many amphibians.

SIZE: 1–1.7 in. long

EGGS: The female lays 200 eggs or more, either singly or in small clusters

FOUND IN: Pine forests and sandhills adjacent to freshwater wetlands

PEREGRINE FALCON
(Falco peregrinus)

The peregrine falcon is the fastest animal on the planet. When diving after prey from above, it can reach speeds of more than 200 miles per hour. For comparison, the cheetah, which is the fastest land mammal, can reach speeds of up to about 65 miles per hour.

In the mid-1900s, peregrine falcons were almost pushed to extinction in the lower forty-eight states. This was due to a pesticide named DDT, which was sprayed from planes mainly to control mosquitoes. Fortunately, this pesticide was banned in 1972. Scientists found that it was harming many animals, not just mosquitoes. Birds of prey, like falcons and eagles, were hit particularly hard.

Since the banning of DDT, peregrine falcon numbers have rebounded. This is partly due to the Endangered Species Act of 1973, as well as efforts by scientists and conservation groups. In fact, they have recovered so much that in 1999 they were taken off the endangered species list.

SIZE: 16 in. long; 3.5 ft. wingspan

DIET: Mostly birds; sometimes small mammals

FOUND IN: A wide diversity of settings—most frequently along mountains ranges, river valleys, and coastlines; they have adapted to nesting in cities

NEW MEXICO

New Mexico is the fourth-ranked state based on biodiversity. It has over 4,500 plant and animal species. This is mostly due to the state's large size (the fifth-largest in the U.S.), in addition to having a diversity of ecotypes. Much of the state is quite arid. This is true in both the deserts of eastern New Mexico and the Rocky Mountains in the west.

GAMBEL OAK
(Quercus gambelii)

The gambel oak grows almost only in the "four corner" states: Utah, Colorado, Arizona, and New Mexico. Gambel oak is adapted to wildfires and will quickly resprout from its roots if a wildfire kills it.

Gambel oaks don't grow very large, but they are one of the hardiest of all oaks. They are able to survive well in areas that have rocky soils, heavy winds, and lots of snow, fire, and drought. They tend to grow in dense colonies. As a result, they often provide wildlife with an abundant source of acorns.

HEIGHT: 20–40 ft.

FOUND IN: A range of settings in mountain foothills

SEASON: Flowers in early spring; drops acorns in the fall

SOAPTREE YUCCA
(Yuca elata)

The soaptree yucca gets its name because some indigenous communities use substances in its roots and trunks as soap. They also use the leaf fibers to make many items. These include baskets, sandals, belts, mats, cords, and more.

As each soaptree yucca tree grows taller, its older leaves die and fold downward along the trunk. This surrounds the trunk in a thatch-like coat, which provides protection to the trunk from excessive heat or cold, and from insects, too.

HEIGHT: 10–25 ft.

FOUND IN: Deserts, mesas, and dry grassland

SEASON: Flowers in late spring to early summer

TREE CHOLLA
(Cylindropuntia imbricata)

The tree cholla, also known as the "cane cholla," is a hardy cactus important for many animals. In particular, cactus wrens and Gila woodpeckers nest in, and on, them. Many small mammals and birds feed on their seeds.

When in bloom, the tree cholla has beautiful pink or purple flowers. In addition to providing nectar to a number of pollinators, these flowers turn into yellow/orange fruits. These fruits can remain attached on the plant for months, and are eaten by a range of wildlife.

HEIGHT: 3–15 ft.

FOUND IN: Arid grasslands, scrublands, and woodlands

SEASON: Flowers mid-spring to mid-summer; fruits ripen mid-summer well into the fall

WHOLELEAF PAINTBRUSH
(Castilleja integra)

The flowers of the wholeleaf paintbrush produce a lot of nectar, which attracts a huge number of hummingbirds, its main pollinators. Several species of hummingbirds feed from these flowers, and in doing so, often pollinate the plants.

Wholeleaf paintbrush relies partly on nearby plants for the nutrients it needs to grow well. Its roots will penetrate the roots of these other plants (often grasses) in order to get those nutrients. When you buy wholeleaf paintbrush plants from a nursery, you will often find them sharing the pot with another plant.

HEIGHT: 12–16 in.

FOUND IN: Arid rocky slopes, prairies, mesas, and woodlands

SEASON: Flowers throughout the summer in most areas, but this can vary dramatically depending upon the location

NEW MEXICO

MULE DEER
(Odocoileus hemionus)

The mule deer was named for its large ears, which look like those of mules, and is an icon of the western U.S., found throughout much of the region. In winter, it often herds in large numbers. In many areas, mule deer migrate seasonally, moving between their summer feeding grounds and their wintering grounds. These migrations can exceed 100 miles and often remain consistent for many generations. It's believed that mothers pass down these migration routes through generations.

SIZE: 3–3.5 ft. tall at the shoulder; 4–7 ft. long

FOUND IN: Relatively open, arid, rocky areas

DIET: A variety of high-quality plant material, including forbs, and the leaves and twigs of woody plants, berries, and fruit

GREATER ROADRUNNER
(Geococcyx californianus)

Greater roadrunners spend most of their lives on the ground. They walk rapidly, searching for prey, before sprinting after it very quickly. They can run upwards of 20 miles per hour during these short hunting sprints. They also sometimes jump straight up into the air to catch flying prey—mostly insects, but sometimes hummingbirds too.

To avoid overheating, roadrunners limit their feeding to the mornings and late afternoons/evenings in spring through fall, spending the hottest part of the day in the shade. At colder times of the day, and during the winter, they bask in the sun to warm up.

SIZE: 20–24 in. long; 1.5–2 ft. wingspan

FOUND IN: Deserts, scrublands, and arid grasslands

DIET: Mostly a variety of larger invertebrates, as well as lizards, snakes, small mammals, small birds, fruits, and seeds

NEW MEXICO SPADEFOOT TOAD
(Spea multiplicata)

The New Mexico spadefoot toad has a spade-like growth on the bottom of each of its hind feet, used to burrow underground. This is how it gets the name "spadefoot." These toads spend most of their life underground, a behavioral adaptation that keeps them from drying out in the hot, dry desert. They emerge some nights to feed and will also emerge during monsoon-season rains to breed. They lay their eggs in pools of the water that form after these rains. The eggs and tadpoles develop quickly—they must grow into toadlets before the pools dry up.

SIZE: 2–2.5 in. long

EGGS: The female lays eggs in small clusters, averaging 1,000 eggs per female

FOUND IN: A wide range of open settings, as long as they have sandy and/or loose soil to burrow into

RAINBOW GRASSHOPPER
(Dactylotum bicolor)

The rainbow grasshopper, also called the "painted grasshopper," is a very colorful creature. Its color pattern varies depending on where you are in its range, but combinations include black, red, orange, purple, yellow, and blue. Bright colors in many animals warn predators of toxicity, but the rainbow grasshopper is not actually toxic. Still, it is not very tasty to most predators, so its bright colors are likely a warning of that.

SIZE: 1.4 in. long (females); 0.8 in. long (males)

EGGS: The female lays up to 12 batches of eggs (with around 100 eggs per batch) in the soil

FOUND IN: Open settings, including shortgrass prairie, desert grasslands, and other sparsely vegetated areas

New York

New York is the largest of the northeastern states. It also has the greatest combined diversity of plants and animals. Much of inland New York is forested, contains a diversity of elevations, and is quite rural. New York also has a fair amount of coastline. This includes Long Island's saltwater coasts and the freshwater coasts of Lakes Ontario and Erie.

AMERICAN CHESTNUT
(Castanea dentata)

The American chestnut used to be widespread in the eastern U.S., including much of the Appalachian Mountains. They made up twenty-five percent of its trees until the early 1900s, when chestnut blight was accidentally introduced from Japan. This came from Japanese chestnut trees imported to the U.S. The fungus killed 3–4 billion American chestnut trees in the U.S., and today they are incredibly rare. Almost all American chestnuts that try to grow in the wild in the U.S. today are unable to grow much beyond the sapling stage before they are killed by the blight. Many organizations are testing genetic strains of American chestnut trees. They hope to find one that can survive in the wild in its historic U.S. range.

HEIGHT: 80–100 ft. (before the chestnut blight was introduced)

SEASON: Flowers late spring to early summer; drops nuts in early fall

FOUND IN: Areas with moderately dry soils, mostly in the Appalachian Mountains

NORTHERN SEASIDE GOLDENROD
(Solidago sempervirens)

The northern seaside goldenrod is one of over a hundred U.S. goldenrod species. It often gets the undeserved blame for causing hay fever, which is actually caused by a different plant: ragweed. Ragweed blooms at the same time and in the same places as goldenrods.

Northern seaside goldenrod is a very important plant. It provides late summer and early fall nectar to many insects, and is a main food source for monarch butterflies on their migration down the east coast to their overwintering grounds.

HEIGHT: 3–6 ft.

SEASON: Flowers late summer into mid-fall

FOUND IN: Open coastal habitats such as dunes, back edges of salt marshes, and open pine woodlands

WHITE SNAKEROOT
(Ageratina altissima)

Early colonists thought white snakeroot could treat snake bites, which is how it got its name. The reality is quite different. This plant is highly toxic to people, even if only ingested through the milk of cows that have eaten it. In the early 1800s, thousands in the Midwest died from this, including Abraham Lincoln's mother.

White snakeroot is also toxic to cows, goats, horses, and sheep, so ranchers and others who raise these animals watch for this plant. They want to be sure it is not in their fields.

HEIGHT: 2–4 ft.

SEASON: Flowering late summer well into fall, it is among the latest of wildflowers to bloom in many areas

FOUND IN: Moist and partially shaded open woodlands and thickets

New York

FISHER
(*Pekania pennanti*)

The fisher is a large member of the weasel family. These are mostly solitary, except for when a female is raising her young (which are called "kits"). Fishers are rarely seen, even where they are common, as they spend most of their time in trees. They have partially retractable claws, which help them to be very agile climbers, and wide feet that help them walk better in deep snow. Often, the most effective way to identify their presence is to look for their tracks in the snow or in mud.

SIZE: 2 ft. long (females); 3 ft. long (males)

DIET: A wide range of smaller mammals, birds, and also nuts, berries, and fruits

FOUND IN: Large tracts of old forests, mostly coniferous or mixed deciduous-coniferous

BARRED OWL
(*Strix varia*)

The barred owl is one of the most readily encountered owls within much of its range. It is more often heard than seen. Its loud and very distinctive call is unmistakable—it sounds like: "Who cooks for you? Who cooks for you all?".

Like many owls, the barred owl doesn't migrate seasonally, but instead stays in the same general area year-round. It is active mainly at night, which is when it does much of its hunting. Although it is one of the bigger owls in the U.S., another owl, the great horned owl, is one of its major predators.

SIZE: 1.5–2 ft. long, 3.5 ft. wingspan, 1.5 ft.

DIET: Mostly small mammals, but also amphibians and, occasionally, crayfish and crabs

FOUND IN: Forests and woodlands with water in or near them

EASTERN NEWT
(Notophthalmus viridescens)

The eastern newt, or "red-spotted newt," is unique among most amphibians, having three life phases. During the first phase, it hatches from its egg and spends several months as an aquatic larva. Then, it emerges from the wetland as a bright-orange juvenile—a "red eft." It spends a few years in the woods in this second phase. Then, for the final phase of its life, it transforms into an aquatic adult, olive green in color, with red spots and a yellow belly. It then returns to a permanent body of water to spend its remaining years there.

SIZE: 3–5 in. long

EGGS: The female lays 200–400 eggs in small clusters, often curled up burrito-style in leaves at the bottom of wetlands

FOUND IN: Forests with permanent freshwater wetlands, either in them or immediately adjacent

KARNER BLUE BUTTERFLY
(Lycaeides melissa samuelis)

The Karner blue butterfly is one of the rarest butterflies in the U.S. Due to habitat shrinkage, its numbers declined sharply in the 1970s and 1980s, and it has been listed as endangered by the U.S. Fish and Wildlife Service since 1992. Its caterpillars feed only on the wild lupine plant, meaning they need a particular habitat.

Karner blue butterfly caterpillars have a mutually beneficial relationship with ants. The caterpillars produce a sugary substance that the ants eat. In return, the ants protect the caterpillars from predators.

SIZE: 1 in. wingspan

EGGS: The female lays 10–80 eggs on, or near, lupine plants

FOUND IN: A variety of open settings (such as prairies, pine barrens, and dunes) that contain wild lupine

NORTH CAROLINA

North Carolina ranks ninth among all fifty states in terms of biodiversity. A vast diversity of ecotypes in the state, particularly coastal habitats on the state's eastern side, means that many species can flourish. As you go east to west in the state, elevation climbs, and you move from coastal plains to grasslands and prairies, then on to forests and then to mountains.

RIVER BIRCH
(Betula nigra)

River birch can be quite easily identified by its peeling bark. Along the entire trunk, many large sections of bark curl and peel back on themselves. This peeling bark is particularly exaggerated during the tree's earlier years.

The color of river birch's bark changes throughout its life. The bark of young trees tends to be a salmon-pinkish color. Then, as the trees age, their bark tends to shift to a darker red or brown. Relatively old trees may eventually attain a dark gray and/or a near-black color.

HEIGHT: 50–70 ft.

SEASON: Flowers in early spring, releases seeds in late spring

FOUND IN: Areas with moist soils, including along riverbanks and streambanks, in floodplain forests, and lake margins

MAPLELEAF VIBURNUM
(Viburnum acerifolium)

As you might have guessed, the leaves of this plant are shaped like the leaves of maple trees, with three sharp-pointed lobes. In fact, many people who see this low-growing shrub often assume it is a young maple seedling.

Mapleleaf viburnum grows mostly in heavy shade underneath dense tree canopies. When it grows in dense colonies, it provides good cover for birds that nest on the forest floor. Its flowers also make nectar, which many pollinators can feed on, and its fruits are eaten by various animals.

HEIGHT: 4–6 ft.

SEASON: Flowers mid-spring through mid-summer; berries ripen late summer and can last into the winter

FOUND IN: Partially shaded areas in woodlands, forests, and wooded hillslopes

CAROLINA LILY
(Lilium michauxii)

The Carolina lily is the state wildflower of North Carolina. It is unique as the only native fragrant lily east of the Rockies in the U.S. This is why people often plant them in their wildflower gardens.

One of the main reasons plants have fragrant flowers is to attract pollinators. This is indeed the case with the Carolina lily. Its flowers attract a range of pollinators, most notably species of swallowtail butterfly.

HEIGHT: 2–4 ft.

SEASON: Flowers mid-summer into late summer

FOUND IN: Dry upland forests, thickets, and ridges

AZURE BLUET
(Houstonia caerulea)

Azure bluets, more often referred to simply as "bluets," add a lovely dash of color to many lawns. They often pop up as patches of many small and delicate flowers. The reason they are mostly seen on lawns is because they don't compete well with other plants. To best seed them in your yard, spread the seeds in partially shady, bare areas with no competing plants. Rock gardens are often a perfect spot for them.

HEIGHT: 6–12 in.

SEASON: Flowers mid-spring through early summer

FOUND IN: Areas of light shade, with minimal other plants present

NORTH CAROLINA

SOUTHERN FLYING SQUIRREL
(Glaucomys volans)

The southern flying squirrel doesn't technically "fly," but rather it glides. It has a folded layer of loose skin between its front and back legs that it spreads out to use for gliding. To get started, these squirrels will jump from a tree branch, and from there can glide upwards of 150 feet away from the tree. They can therefore move between trees that are far apart, or quickly go from the upper part of a tree down to the ground.

Southern flying squirrels are only active at night, when their big eyes help them see clearly in the dark.

SIZE: 8–10 in. long

DIET: Mostly a variety of nuts, seeds, berries, fungi, and insects

FOUND IN: Forests containing an abundance of large deciduous trees

GREAT BLUE HERON
(Ardea herodias)

The great blue heron is often seen feeding in the shallow areas along the edges of wetlands. These are very stealthy hunters, staying still for long periods of time as they wait for their prey to come to them. Very quickly, they will then stab their prey with their long bills.

Great blue herons often nest in large colonies, which sometimes contain over a hundred adults. They build large nests out of sticks toward the tops of trees. These trees are often in, or very close to, wetlands.

SIZE: 4 ft. long; 6 ft. wingspan

DIET: Mostly fish, but also amphibians, reptiles, invertebrates, and small mammals

FOUND IN: Edges of fresh and saltwater marshes, swamps, rivers, ponds, and lakes

MARBLED SALAMANDER
(*Ambystoma opacum*)

Like many amphibians, female marbled salamanders lay their eggs in temporary freshwater wetlands. Most years, these wetlands will dry up, typically during late spring or summer, which means that fish can't live in them. This is important because fish are the major predators of amphibians.

The marbled salamander is unique, laying its eggs in late summer rather than spring, as other amphibians do. She lays them on the ground in a dried-up part of the wetland. After the female has done this, she will remain with her eggs, keeping them safe from predators and making sure they stay moist. Later, when the pond has filled up enough to cover the eggs, typically in the fall, the female returns to the woods, soon after which the eggs will hatch, and the aquatic larvae that are born will overwinter in the pond. By next spring, when other amphibians lay their eggs, the marbled salamander larvae will be quite large. The species takes advantage of this head start and feeds on the larvae of the other amphibian species.

SIZE: 3–5 in. long

EGGS: The female lays between 50 and 200 eggs

FOUND IN: Damp forests and woodlands containing a vernal pool or pools

North Dakota

The nineteenth-largest state, North Dakota is relatively remote and unpopulated, but ranks forty-eighth among all fifty states for biodiversity. This low species diversity is mostly due to two factors. Of the lower forty-eight states, it is one of the northernmost and is also very arid. Even so, there are still lots of interesting animals and plants that live in North Dakota.

PEACHLEAF WILLOW
(Salix amygdaloides)

The peachleaf willow is a quick-growing tree. In a single year, it can grow between 3 and 10 feet taller. However, it is relatively short-lived for a tree. It can live up to about seventy-five years old, though many don't survive that long.

Peachleaf willow branches are flexible and strong. Because of this, indigenous communities have used them to make many items, including baskets, backrests for chairs, drying racks, fishing traps, and much more.

HEIGHT: 15–70 ft.

FOUND IN: A wide range of settings with moist soils

SEASON: Flowers in mid-spring; fruits in late spring and early summer

WILD PRAIRIE ROSE
(Rosa arkansana)

The wild prairie rose is the state flower of North Dakota. When in bloom, it has beautiful pink flowers, which survive well even in droughts. This is because of the flower's very deep roots.

Many animals, like birds, deer, antelope, and skunks, eat the fruit of wild prairie rose plants. These fruits are known as "rose hips" and are full of nutrients, including a high concentration of vitamin C.

HEIGHT: 1–3 ft.

SEASON: Flowers late spring through summer

FOUND IN: A wide range of open settings, including prairies, open woodlands, and savannas

UPRIGHT PRAIRIE CONEFLOWER
(Ratibida columnifera)

The upright prairie coneflower is sometimes called the "Mexican hat flower," since it is shaped a bit like a sombrero. The tall part in the middle, named the "column," is made up of many florets, which bloom at the bottom of the column first, and move up as summer progresses. Many people plant these in their wildflower gardens because of their interesting and colorful flowers, as well as their lovely fragrance.

HEIGHT: 1–3 ft.

SEASON: Flowers late spring through summer

FOUND IN: Prairies and open, disturbed areas like roadsides and pastures

SILVER BUFFALOBERRY
(Shepherdia argentea)

The silver buffaloberry is very popular among birds. Its branches grow densely together and have sizable thorns on them, making it a great protective cover for birds to nest and take refuge from predators in. The birds, especially the sharp-tailed grouse, also like the silver buffaloberry for its fruits. The berries are also eaten by humans, who have historically used them to flavor bison meat.

HEIGHT: 6–16 ft.

SEASON: Flowers in early to mid-spring; fruits ripen in late summer

FOUND IN: A wide diversity of settings: along rivers, in woodlands, along prairie slopes, and even dry plains

North Dakota

THIRTEEN-LINED GROUND SQUIRREL
(Ictidomys tridecemlineatus)

As you'll likely have guessed, these ground squirrels have thirteen stripes running down their body. They will either have seven wide dark-brown stripes, alternating with six narrow tan ones, or seven narrow yellow stripes, alternating with six wide dark-brown ones.

Thirteen-lined ground squirrels live in underground burrows. They are active aboveground during the day, when they keep their burrows open. At night, they plug the entrance and stay inside. They are one of those rare animals that hibernates during the winter, and for this they have a separate hibernation burrow, below where the frost can get to it—sometimes more than 3 feet underground!

SIZE: 8–12 in. long

DIET: Grasses, herbaceous plants, seeds, and crops. Also worms, insects, small birds, and lizards

FOUND IN: Prairies and other areas covered by short grasses and herbaceous plants

BLUE-WINGED TEAL
(Spatula discors)

Blue-winged teal are named for the large, powder-blue patch on the leading edge of their wings. This patch is mostly only visible when they are in flight. They are the second-most abundant duck in North America. Only the mallard is more populous.

The blue-winged teal is a warm-weather duck, more so than most North American ducks. Many of them migrate to wintering grounds in South America, starting in early fall, without returning to their breeding grounds in the U.S. until late spring.

SIZE: 14–16 in. long; 2 ft. wingspan

DIET: Seeds, aquatic vegetation, and small aquatic invertebrates

FOUND IN: Shallow freshwater wetlands and neighboring grasslands

PAINTED TURTLE
(Chrysemys picta)

Painted turtles are found in almost any freshwater wetland in their range, as long as there are some sunny spots for them to bask in. They are even found in some brackish wetlands. They bask to warm up their body temperature, as well as to get rid of leeches.

The male has much longer front claws than the female, which he uses in courtship rituals, waving them at the female and stroking her head with the back of them.

SIZE: 3–10 in. long

EGGS: The female lays 5–6 eggs underground, and will sometimes nest twice in a year

FOUND IN: A wide range of freshwater wetlands with some sun exposure

BROWN-BELTED BUMBLEBEE
(Bombus griseocollis)

Brown-belted bumblebees live in colonies, each with one queen. After she emerges from overwintering, the queen builds a nest site, where over the next several months she lays her eggs and raises young. Most of these eggs turn into workers who help raise the young, protect the colony, and gather food and water. In late summer, some males and future queens will hatch from the eggs. They will leave the colony in the fall and mate with others from nearby colonies. The newly hatched queens will be the only ones to survive and overwinter, allowing the cycle to begin again.

SIZE: 0.75–1 in. long (queens); 0.3–0.5 in. long (males/workers)

EGGS: 50 eggs per female

FOUND IN: A diversity of setting ranging from grasslands and meadows to suburban yards, and even urban settings

OHIO

Much of western and northern Ohio is comprised of plains, whereas the eastern half of the state is quite hilly. Several sizable rivers run through Ohio. Many drain from Lake Erie, which forms about two-thirds of the state's northern border. Ohio ranks twenty-seventh in the U.S. for plant and animal diversity, with over 3,000 documented species.

OHIO BUCKEYE
(Aesculus glabra)

The Ohio buckeye is the state tree of Ohio, named for its seed, which resembles a deer's eye. The tree is so significant to the state that people from Ohio are nicknamed "buckeyes." It also is the mascot for Ohio State University.

Ohio buckeye seeds are poisonous to cattle and to humans, though a variety of other species can eat them. The tannic acid in them has long been used by indigenous people to tan leather hides. Indigenous communities have also ground the seeds to poison the fish in streams, collecting them when they float to the surface.

HEIGHT: Typically 30–50 ft., but up to 75 ft.

FOUND IN: Floodplains and rich, moist woodlands, among other settings

SEASON: Flowers in early to mid-spring; nuts drop in early fall

COMMON HACKBERRY
(Celtis occidentalis)

The common hackberry is a tree whose cork-like bark has somewhat warty-looking protuberances. For a long time, scientists thought that its closest relative was the elm, but in around 2009 they found that, in fact, it is more closely related to plants in the cannabis family.

Many birds feed on the abundance of berries produced by the common hackberry, and the caterpillars of several butterfly species develop on its leaves. As a result, this tree is a good choice for planting in wildlife-friendly yards.

HEIGHT: 60–80 ft.

SEASON: Flowers in mid-spring; fruits ripen in late summer/early fall

FOUND IN: Areas alongside rivers and streams, most commonly, but also rocky hillsides, open woodlands, and sand barrens

GREAT WHITE TRILLIUM
(Trilium grandiflorum)

The seeds of the great white trillium have a fascinating dispersal mechanism. Attached to the seeds is a fleshy packet containing a large quantity of oleic acid, the same substance emitted by dead ants. This causes nearby ants to carry the seeds away, to a central location underground. This keeps the seeds safe from animals that might otherwise eat them, and also provides a great microclimate for germination. From here, a new colony of great white trillium can form.

HEIGHT: 1–1.5 ft.

SEASON: Flowers in mid-spring

FOUND IN: Deciduous and mixed deciduous/coniferous forests with rich soils

CARDINAL FLOWER
(Lobelia cardinalis)

The cardinal flower is a popular choice for wildflower gardens. People plant it to attract hummingbirds. When in full bloom, these flowers are covered in bright-red tubular flowers—magnets to hungry hummingbirds. Each plant grows a tall stalk from which the flowers bloom, starting from the bottom and moving upward over several weeks. Many butterflies, especially swallowtails, are drawn to these flowers.

HEIGHT: 2–5 ft.

SEASON: Flowers late summer into early/mid-fall

FOUND IN: Areas with moist soils, including along edges of wetlands and in low woodlands

OHIO

BOBCAT
(Lynx rufus)

The bobcat is named for its short, or "bobbed," tail. These are found throughout much of the lower forty-eight states, aside from a good portion of the upper Midwest. Even in areas where they are relatively common, these animals are rarely seen, mainly because they are wary of people.

Often the best way to document bobcats in an area is to look for their tracks in the mud or snow, or for their "scat" (poop). They often mark their territory by depositing their scat and/or urinating on exposed, elevated surfaces like logs, rocks, or stumps.

SIZE: 2.5–3 ft. long; 18–22 in. tall at the shoulder

DIET: Rabbits, squirrels, rodents, skunks, opossums, birds, and snakes

FOUND IN: Mostly forested areas, around swamps, and suburban areas with sizable woodland tracts

HELLBENDER
(Cryptobranchus alleganiensis)

The hellbender is the largest salamander in the U.S., and the third-largest salamander in the world. The largest is the South China giant salamander, which can grow to almost 6 feet long and weighs around 100 pounds!

Hellbenders live their entire life on the bottom of rivers and large streams. They spend most of their time under large rocks, where they sit and wait for prey they can ambush. At night, they come out to actively hunt along the river bottom, mostly for crayfish. Their thick, wrinkled skin helps their bodies absorb oxygen from the water.

SIZE: 1–2.5 ft. long

EGGS: The female lays 100–500 eggs, in a nest made by the male, under a large rock on the bottom of the river

FOUND IN: Clean, cool, swift-running streams and rivers

NORTHERN WALKINGSTICK
(Diapheromera femorata)

Adult northern walkingsticks are very well camouflaged to blend in with tree canopies, where they spend most of their adult life.

From the tree canopy, the female drops her eggs to the ground, each one surrounded by a substance that is tasty to ants. Ants will then often bring the eggs to their nest underground. They eat the surrounding substance, leaving the egg, unharmed, in a waste pile. The walkingstick egg then develops there, typically over the winter, safely underground. In the spring, after hatching, the young walkingsticks will emerge back aboveground.

SIZE: 3–4 in. long

EGGS: The female drops about 150 eggs from trees in the fall, which overwinter in leaf litter and hatch in the spring

FOUND IN: A wide range of deciduous woodlands and forests

Oklahoma

Oklahoma contains quite a diversity of habitats. This includes prairies, plains, forests, wetlands, caves, and sand dunes, among others. In general, as you go from east to west in Oklahoma, the elevation rises. Almost the entire western third of Oklahoma is over 2,000 feet high. Its highest point, at 4,972 feet, is near the western border.

BLACKJACK OAK
(Quercus marilandica)

The blackjack oak is a very hardy tree. It is able to grow in low-nutrient soils where many other woody plants cannot, and can even survive fire, mainly thanks to its thick bark.

This tree has quite unique-looking bark, which often grows in somewhat rectangular blocks. Some people say it reminds them of alligator skin. The shape of the blackjack oak's leaves can be quite variable, but are always distinct. They are narrow at the base, broadening out into three subtly defined lobes, quite like the suit of clubs on playing cards.

HEIGHT: 30–50 ft.

SEASON: Flowers in mid-spring; acorns fall in early/mid-fall

FOUND IN: Areas with sandy soils, as well as dry slopes and ridges

AMERICAN MISTLETOE
(Phoradendron leucarpum)

American mistletoe is a parasitic plant. It grows on the branches or trunks of trees, penetrating them with their roots and stealing nutrients and water. Eventually, if the mistletoe spreads widely enough, it will end up killing the tree.

Mistletoes are well known for their use as a decoration during the holiday season. Tradition says that two people who find themselves under the mistletoe must kiss, though it's not entirely clear where the tradition came from.

HEIGHT: Up to 3 ft. (stem)

SEASON: Fruits ripen late fall/early winter

FOUND IN: Grows on most types of deciduous tree in its range

TALL THISTLE
(Cirsium altissimum)

The tall thistle is a member of the sunflower family. It is very important to various forms of wildlife, with bees, butterflies, and moths feeding on its nectar. It is the larval host for the swamp metalmark butterfly—a rare species in Oklahoma and its surrounding states.

Many birds also feed on the seeds of this plant, particularly the American goldfinch, which times its nesting to coincide with when thistle seeds will be available to feed to its young. As a result, these birds nest later than most, often starting in late summer.

HEIGHT: 3–10 ft.

SEASON: Flowers late summer/early fall

FOUND IN: Prairies, open woodlands, and disturbed sites

CORALBERRY
(Symphoricarpos orbiculatus)

Coralberry, or "buckbrush," is in the honeysuckle family. Its leaves are heavily grazed by white-tailed deer, which is how it got its nickname. It tends to grow as a dense thicket, which a lot of birds like because it provides a relatively safe place to nest in. It is also a host plant for some types of hummingbird moths. Some people plant them in wildflower gardens, hoping to attract these interesting creatures.

HEIGHT: 2–5 ft.

SEASON: Flowers late spring/early summer; fruits ripen mid-fall

FOUND IN: A variety of woodlands, especially near/along edges; also thickets and banks of streams and rivers

Oklahoma

LONG-TAILED WEASEL
(Mustela frenata)

Though rather small, the long-tailed weasel is a mighty predator, often taking down prey several times its own size.

Most of the year, long-tailed weasels are brown on top and on their sides, and their bellies are either white or yellowish. In some, mostly northern, areas, their coat is entirely white during the winter, except for a black tail tip. This helps them better camouflage in snowy landscapes.

SIZE: 1–1.5 ft. long

DIET: Mainly small mammals such as mice and voles, but also squirrels, chipmunks, birds and their eggs, fruits, and berries

FOUND IN: Open woodlands, shrublands, and meadows; most frequently encountered near forest-field edges

SCISSOR-TAILED FLYCATCHER
(Tyrannus forficatus)

There's no way you could confuse a scissor-tailed flycatcher with any other bird. Their extremely long, forked "tails" (they are not actually tails, but long feathers) are unmistakable. Tail length averages 8–9 inches for males, and 6 for females.

Thanks to their special tail, scissor-tailed flycatchers are very maneuverable fliers. This comes in handy when they're hunting flying insects.

SIZE: 10–14 in. long; 6 in. wingspan; 10 in. tail length (females), 15 in. (males)

DIET: Mostly flying insects; some berries and fruits, mainly during the winter

FOUND IN: Open areas with scattered trees and/or shrubs

EASTERN COLLARED LIZARD
(Crotaphytus collaris)

The eastern collared lizard is the state reptile of Oklahoma. The males are very colorful. They have bright blue-green bodies with yellow stripes on their bodies and tails, and often a bright yellowish-orange head and neck. Females are more drably colored, but during the breeding season the orange spots on their head and body become brighter.

The eastern collared lizard can run very fast—as fast as 16 miles per hour! Sometimes they even run on their hind legs.

SIZE: 8–15 in. long (including the tail)

FOUND IN: Open, arid locations with abundant rocks, boulders, and rocky outcrops

EGGS: The female lays 4–12 eggs, sometimes two clutches of eggs in a year

COMMON BUCKEYE
(Junonia coenia)

The common buckeye is a butterfly with notable circular spots on its wings called "eyespots." These are reminiscent of the nuts of the Ohio buckeye tree, which is how the common buckeye got its name. The eyespots are thought to fool predators, who think they really are eyes.

Common buckeyes aren't tolerant of cold weather. Those in the northern parts of their range migrate southward during the first cold fronts of early fall.

SIZE: 2–2.5 in. long; 1.5–2.5 in. wingspan

FOUND IN: Almost any vegetated open areas, including meadows, fields, pastures, yards, and parks

EGGS: The female lays eggs individually on host plant leaves

OREGON

Much of Oregon is covered by mountains, including twenty peaks that exceed 9,000 feet in elevation! The state has vast forests, high grasslands, and rangeland. It also has extensive valleys and a long ocean coastline. Thanks to its large size and diverse habitats, Oregon is richly biodiverse, with more than 4,000 plant and animal species in the state.

DOUGLAS FIR
(Pseudotsuga menziesii)

The Douglas fir, often referred to as "Doug fir," is the state tree of Oregon. It is one of the most valuable timber trees in the United States. Its wood has many uses—for furniture, poles, fences, flooring, and more. Even with all these uses, the Douglas fir is still most commonly known as a Christmas tree.

The Douglas fir is not actually a fir, nor is it a pine, spruce, or hemlock, though it shares characteristics with a number of trees. Its genus, "Pseudotsuga," means "false hemlock tree."

Douglas fir trees can be very long-lived, frequently making it to 500 years old, with some living upwards of 1,000 years. They are very fire resistant, and they are often the first trees to grow back after wildfires. They provide important habitats to a wide variety of wildlife, including the federally threatened northern spotted owl.

HEIGHT: 250–300 ft.; (5–12 ft. diameter)

SEASON: Leafy year-round

FOUND IN: A wide range of settings, most often along moist, coastal areas in the Pacific Northwest and subalpine mountain slopes in the Rocky Mountains

OREGON GRAPE
(Berberis aquifolium)

The Oregon grape is the state flower of Oregon. Its name is a bit of a misnomer, as it is actually a type of barberry, though its fruits, which are blue-black berries, do resemble grapes. It is less commonly known as the "holly-leaved barberry," as its leaves look like those of holly plants, and are also evergreen. Though seedy and sour, lots of fruit-eating birds and mammals eat this plant's berries.

HEIGHT: 3–10 ft. tall

SEASON: Flowers in early to mid-spring; fruits ripen beginning in early summer

FOUND IN: The understory of coniferous forests and in shrublands

PACIFIC TRILLIUM
(Trillium ovatum)

The Pacific trillium is one of the most abundant and widespread trilliums in the Pacific Northwest. It spreads underground through extensive root systems known as "rhizomes." The flowers typically bloom white and become pink as time goes on. In the Smith River Canyon of southern Oregon and northern California, their flowers turn a red-brown color.

Individual Pacific trillium plants don't grow above ground every year. When they don't, this is known as "dormancy." Pacific trillium plants usually won't go dormant for more than a year or two, but some have gone dormant for up to five years in a row.

HEIGHT: 10–18 in.

SEASON: Flowers from late winter to early spring

FOUND IN: Shady woodlands, moist woodland slopes, and stream banks

OREGON

YELLOW-BELLIED MARMOT
(Marmota flaviventris)

The yellow-bellied marmot is closely related to the woodchuck, but the two species differ in some important ways. Both live in burrows that they dig themselves, however yellow-bellied marmots live in colonies of up to twenty, while woodchucks tend to live alone. Woodchucks mostly live in low elevations, typically meadows and fields. Yellow-bellied marmots, by contrast, live in hilly and mountainous areas, making their burrows along the slopes. Both species are true hibernators. In some locales, yellow-bellied marmots hibernate for up to eight months straight.

SIZE: 18–27 in. long

DIET: Grasses, forbs, and seeds of flowers

FOUND IN: Open habitats such as pastures, alpine meadows, hill/mountain slopes, and forest edges

GOLDEN EAGLE
(Aquila chrysaetos)

In addition to being the largest eagle in the United States, the golden eagle is an impressive flier, spending much of its flight time gliding on long, broad wings, at speeds of around 30 miles per hour. As these birds glide, seemingly effortlessly, their wings are elevated slightly upward, giving them a subtle V-shape. When the eagle dives in the air (called "stooping") after prey, its wings angle downward, and it holds its legs against its tail, tucking the wings tight to the body. When diving, the golden eagle can reach speeds of up to 200 miles per hour. That's almost as fast as the peregrine falcon, making the golden eagle the second-fastest animal in the world!

SIZE: 2.5 ft. long; 6–7 ft. wingspan

DIET: Mostly rabbits, hares, ground squirrels, and prairie dogs, but also birds, reptiles, and fish

FOUND IN: Open settings near hills, cliffs, and bluffs

ROUGH-SKINNED NEWT
(Taricha granulosa)

The rough-skinned newt is known for its very strong toxins. When threatened by a potential predator, it assumes a posture known as the "unken reflex," in which it raises its head straight up, turns its tail up over its body, and splays out its legs. This shows off the newt's bright-orange underside, which warns predators of its toxicity.

The toxin that rough-skinned newts produce is known as tetrodotoxin, and is the same toxin found in pufferfish. If eaten by a predator, it can cause paralysis and lead to death.

SIZE: 4–7 in. long (including the tail)

EGGS: The female lays around 500 eggs, individually on underwater stems and leaves

FOUND IN: A variety of freshwater wetlands (for breeding), forested hills, and mountains

WESTERN TIGER SWALLOWTAIL
(Papilio rutulus)

The western tiger swallowtail is named for its black, tiger-like stripes. It is one of the largest butterflies where it is found, and the female is larger than the male. These can often be found at the edges of puddles and on mud, feeding on minerals.

The caterpillars of this species are large and lime-green with two large "eyespots" on their bodies. It's thought that predators believe these are real eyes, which keeps them away.

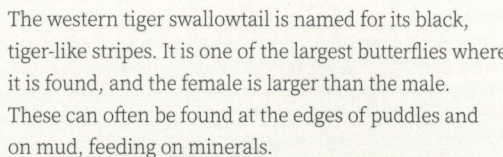

SIZE: 3–4 in. wingspan

EGGS: The female lays up to 100 individual eggs on the leaves of a host plant

FOUND IN: A wide variety of settings, including meadows, wetlands, mountain woodlands, and even urban parks and gardens

Pennsylvania

Much of Pennsylvania is forested. In fact, the "sylvania" part of its name means "forest land" or "woods" in Latin. Pennsylvania is quite hilly, especially the central and northern portions of the state. It is also quite rocky. More than 3,000 plant and animal species call Pennsylvania home.

EASTERN HEMLOCK
(Tsuga canadensis)

The eastern hemlock is a slow-growing tree, as it mainly lives in shady areas and acidic, nutrient-poor soils. The flip side of this is that it can grow to be quite old—upwards of 500 years in some cases.

Eastern hemlock trees are very important for a lot of different wildlife. Their bark and twigs are one of the major sources of winter food for porcupines, and a large number of mammals and birds feed heavily on the seeds within their small cones. Various species use eastern hemlocks for cover from deep snow, including white-tailed deer and ground-feeding birds, like ruffed grouse and wild turkey.

HEIGHT: 50–75 ft.

SEASON: Flowers in mid- to late spring; retains foliage year-round

FOUND IN: Rocky ridges, mountain slopes, and river corridors

PENNGIFT CROWNVETCH
(Coronilla varia)

The penngift crownvetch is Pennsylvania's official "beautification and conservation plant." Its name is a blend of the state's name and the name of the farmer, "Gift," on whose land it was first discovered. The Pennsylvania Department of Transportation has widely planted penngift crownvetch along roadsides in Pennsylvania. This is to control erosion, since the plant grows and spreads into dense a mat. It also has the bonus of pinkish-white flowers that bloom all summer.

HEIGHT: 1–2 ft.

SEASON: Flowers from early summer into the fall

FOUND IN: Widely planted along roadside slopes to reduce erosion

PENNSYLVANIA BLACKBERRY
(Rubus pensilvanicus)

The Pennsylvania blackberry is gorged on by many different mammals in the state, from moose to raccoons and more, as well as more than fifty bird species. People use blackberries to make jelly, pies, and even liquors such as brandy.

Pennsylvania blackberry plants often grow as dense thickets. This, combined with their prickly thorns, makes them great for birds, including for nesting and for protective cover.

HEIGHT: 5–10 ft.

SEASON: Flowers in mid-spring; fruits ripen in mid-summer

FOUND IN: Woodland openings, edges, thickets, meadows, and along fence rows

EASTERN SKUNK CABBAGE
(Symplocarpus foetidus)

Eastern skunk cabbage is one of the first plants to flower each year. It gets the "skunk" part of its name from its powerful odor, which helps to attract its fly pollinators.

The skunk cabbage has a purplish leaf-like structure, called a "spathe." This is the first part to emerge above ground each year, and protects the plant's early flowers from the cold. Inside the spathe, temperatures can be 15–30 degrees warmer than the surrounding air, so some bees and other insects go inside it to warm up.

HEIGHT: 1.5–3 ft.

SEASON: Flowers from late winter to early spring

FOUND IN: Moist woodlands, wetlands, and near streams

Pennsylvania

WHITE-TAILED DEER
(Odocoileus virginianus)

The white-tailed deer is the most abundant and widespread deer in the United States. These are found across the eastern two thirds of the country, and are also widespread west of the Rockies.

Males (known as "bucks") grow antlers each year, which they shed in the winter. These are used to show off a buck's health when he is vying to mate with a female deer, or "doe." White-tailed deer can run very fast—upwards of 30 miles per hour—and can jump as high as 10 feet and as far as 30 feet. When fleeing predators, they flash the underside of their white tails.

SIZE: 3–3.5 ft. tall at the shoulders; 6 ft. long

FOUND IN: A wide range of settings, especially areas where woodlands meet fields

DIET: Primarily live plants in spring and summer; corn, acorns, and other nuts in the fall; buds and twigs of woody plants in winter

COMMON BOX TURTLE
(Terrapene carolina)

The common box turtle has hinges on the bottom of its shell. These enable it to close up completely, kind of like a box, to keep safe from predators. The hinges are so strong that even raccoons can't open them.

Common box turtles are able to live upwards of a hundred years in the wild. They live almost all their lives on land, similar to what many tortoises do. Very occasionally, during really hot, dry conditions, box turtles will seek out water or mud to cool off in; otherwise, you are unlikely to find them in water.

SIZE: 5–7 in. long

EGGS: The female lays 3–8 eggs underground

FOUND IN: Open woodlands, meadows, and shrublands

MONARCH BUTTERFLY
(*Danaus plexippus*)

There are two populations of monarch butterflies in the U.S. One population is found west of the Rocky Mountains and the other to the east.

Most of the eastern population overwinter in high-elevation fir forests in central Mexico, 1.5–2 miles above sea level. In the spring, they begin their northward migration. It takes three generations until some monarchs reach the northeastern U.S. in the summer, meaning the ones who make it that far are the great-grandchildren of the monarch butterflies that left Mexico in the spring. Those butterflies then lay eggs, and the fourth generation (the great-great-grandchildren) emerge as butterflies in late summer. These are the ones that travel all the way to overwinter in Mexico. This last leg of the migration takes place from September to early November. It's a journey of over 2,000 miles, and somehow the butterflies know just where to go!

SIZE: 3–4.5 in. long; 3–4 in. wingspan

EGGS: The female lays 100–300 eggs, individually on milkweed leaves

FOUND IN: Open areas such as prairies, meadows, grasslands, and yards, especially those with milkweed plants

RHODE ISLAND

Rhode Island is the smallest state, which limits its biodiversity. Still, more than 2,000 plant and animal species are found there, thanks to the state's varied habitats. These include varied coastal ecosystems and a diversity of forest types.

RED MAPLE
(Acer rubrum)

The red maple is named for its several different red parts, which include its red flowers, fruits, and twigs, and also its well-known red foliage in the fall. Its leaves can also turn yellow or orange in the fall.

Red maples are abundant in many eastern U.S. forests. They grow fast and thrive in a variety of habitats. Their seeds are contained in an interestingly shaped structure called a "samara." The samara has a seed at one end and a thin, winglike projection at the other. People often call these "helicopters" or "whirlybirds," because they fall in a spiral pattern, especially when caught by the wind.

HEIGHT: 50–90 ft.

SEASON: Flowers in early to mid-spring

FOUND IN: A very wide range of settings, including sunny and shady locations, wet and dry soils, and more

SASSAFRAS
(Sassafras albidum)

Sassafras is well known for its leaf variability. Leaves of Sassafras can have three lobes, two lobes, or be unlobed. Sometimes all three leaf variants can be found on the same branch.

Sassafras roots are often used to make homemade root beer. Their leaves are dried, ground up, and made into filé powder. This is a spicy herb that is used to make gumbo, a popular meal in Louisiana Creole cuisine.

HEIGHT: 30–60 ft.

SEASON: Flowers in early to mid-spring; fruits ripen late summer

FOUND IN: Most any open area with abundant sun exposure, especially in disturbed sites

NORTHERN BAYBERRY
(Morella pensylvanica)

Northern bayberry is an important plant of coastal sand dune ecosystems. Its presence there helps to stabilize the soil and limit landward expansion of the dunes. Some important sand dune plants also grow better with northern bayberry. These include American beachgrass and seaside goldenrod, among others. Northern bayberry helps these plants by increasing soil nitrogen and creating better microclimates for growth, especially in dense thickets.

HEIGHT: 5–10 ft.

SEASON: Flowers in mid-spring; fruits ripen in late summer

FOUND IN: Sandy coastal areas, swampy woods, bogs, and the borders of woodlands

BEACH PEA
(Lathyrus japonicus)

Beach pea most often grows in coastal dunes. It prefers areas with some sand movement, such as the leading edge of the dunes. Frequently, it grows from there up to the back of the beach, as a sprawling vine.

Beach pea is native to four continents: North and South America, Europe, and Asia. The reason for its very widespread distribution is the hardiness of its seeds. These can float, and are able to stay viable for up to five years while in seawater, which allows them to drift extremely far—even across oceans!

HEIGHT: 1–2 ft.

SEASON: Flowers in summer; seed pods mature in late summer

FOUND IN: Sandy and gravelly beaches and leading edges of coastal dunes

RHODE ISLAND

STAR-NOSED MOLE
(Condylura cristata)

The star-nosed mole is named for the star-shaped structure at the end of its snout. This structure is about the size of a human fingertip and is made up of twenty-two fleshy tentacles. The mole uses this to feel for prey, which it hunts underground and sometimes underwater. In total, this structure contains about 100,000 nerve fibers—about five times as many as are in a human hand! This means it can be very sensitive in detecting prey.

SIZE: 6–8 in. long

DIET: A wide range of invertebrates, as well as some small amphibians and small fish

FOUND IN: Areas with moist soil, including marshes, bogs, woodlands, and wet fields

BLUE JAY
(Cyanocitta cristata)

The blue jay is a member of the same family of birds as crows and ravens. These birds are quite vocal, and known to be rather smart. They can even mimic a number of other birds, including hawks.

Their feathers aren't actually blue, but because of the way they are structured, they cause light to scatter in a certain way and look blue to us. Next time you find a blue jay feather, hold it up with the light behind it. You'll realize the feather is actually brown!

SIZE: 11 in. long; 16 in. wingspan

DIET: Mostly nuts, seeds, and fruits

FOUND IN: Oak and pine woodlands, surburban areas, and orchards

EASTERN HOGNOSE SNAKE

(Heterodon platirhinos)

When threatened by a predator, the eastern hognose snake will use several tactics to try and deter it. If fleeing doesn't work,
it will inflate its body and hiss to try to scare the predator away.
Next, it will raise its head and flatten its "hood," like a cobra. Then, it will strike with its head, mouth closed, at the predator. If all this doesn't work, it will play dead, flipping onto its back, vomiting any food, and letting its tongue hang out. If you try
to flip it right side up, it will turn just upside down again.

SIZE: 2–3.5 ft. long

EGGS: The female lays 6–30 eggs in sandy soil and/or under a cover object

FOUND IN: Woodlands with sandy soils, fields, shrublands, and coastal areas

AMERICAN BURYING BEETLE

(Nicrophorus americanus)

The American burying beetle has a fascinating life. After emerging from underground hibernation, the adult beetle starts to hunt for an animal carcass. One about the size of a pigeon is ideal—between 2 and 10 ounces. Once they have found it, a male and female beetle can bury the carcass underground within a single night. After removing all of its fur or feathers, the male and female mate. The female then lays her eggs in the soil next to the carcass. At least one of the parents, usually the female, will stay with the young for a short while after they hatch, feeding them regurgitated food until they can eat the carcass themselves.

SIZE: 1–1.8 in. long

EGGS: Normally 12–18 eggs, but sometimes upwards of 25, laid underground next to a buried carcass

FOUND IN: Grasslands, scrublands, sandy coastal dunes, and forest edges

South Carolina

South Carolina has a wide diversity of ecotypes. These include an abundance of varied coastal environments, plains, sandhills, forests, and wetlands. Elevation generally rises as you move inland from the coast, with the highest elevation in South Carolina reaching just over 3,500 feet along the Blue Ridge Mountains, at the westernmost edge of the state.

SAW PALMETTO
(Serenoa repens)

Saw palmetto is named for the two rows of sharp teeth along the broad stems of its large, fan-shaped leaves. These look like the teeth of a saw blade, and will cut anyone who walks through them in shorts.

Saw palmetto is used by hundreds of different wildlife species, often as cover, given how densely it grows and how much shade it provides. Many animals eat its berries, and the abundant flowers along its long flowering stalk provide nectar to many pollinators. In fact, saw palmetto honey, from bees that feed on the nectar, is a very popular commercial honey.

HEIGHT: 5–10 ft.

FOUND IN: Pine woodlands and scrublands

SEASON: Flowers early to mid-spring; fruits ripen late summer to early fall

CORAL HONEYSUCKLE
(Lonicera sempervirens)

Many people plant coral honeysuckle in their yard, where it can climb fences, archways, and trellises. It often grows as a woody vine and is covered in beautiful red flowers. These tubular red flowers attract hummingbirds and various butterflies. In some warmer areas, coral honeysuckle will keep its leaves year-round, but more commonly it drops its leaves in winter.

HEIGHT: 10–20 ft.

SEASON: Flowers mid-spring, lasting until early fall in many locations; fruits ripen in early fall

FOUND IN: Forest edges, open woodlands, and a range of human-altered settings

MUSCADINE
(Vitis rotundifolia)

Muscadine has the common nickname "grape of the South," and the grapes from its plants are popular for making artisan wines. They also are used to make grape juice, jelly, and hull pie. Dozens of bird species feed on these grapes, as do a variety of other wildlife, including many mammals. These mammals include white-tailed deer, black bears, foxes, rabbits, and squirrels.

Because it grows as a dense vine, many people grow muscadine in their yards along fences and trellises. They are often used as a natural privacy screen, while also serving the added purpose of providing food and cover for lots of wildlife.

HEIGHT: Up to 80 ft.

SEASON: Flowers in mid- to late spring; fruits ripen in early fall

FOUND IN: Open woodlands, coastal sites, and human-altered settings

SPANISH MOSS
(Tillandsia usneoides)

Spanish moss is not actually a moss, but a member of the pineapple family. It is what is known as an "epiphyte"—a plant that grows on other plants but is not parasitic. It absorbs water and nutrients from rainfall and the air. Spanish moss often grows on tree branches, mainly those of southern live oaks and bald cypress trees.

Spanish moss is sensitive to contaminants in the air. As a result, urban areas have seen a decline in it, due to increased air pollution levels.

HEIGHT: Clusters can grow 10–20 ft. long

SEASON: Flowers most often in spring and early summer

FOUND IN: Trees in high humidity areas, often near or in swamps, rivers, and estuaries

South Carolina

EASTERN DIAMONDBACK RATTLESNAKE
(Crotalus adamanteus)

The eastern diamondback rattlesnake gets its name for the diamond pattern that runs the length of its body. It is the longest and heaviest venomous snake in North America. The toxin in its venom causes tissue damage by killing red blood cells.

This snake is a sit-and-wait predator, often lying still along logs or exposed tree roots while waiting for prey. When an object of prey comes by, it strikes quickly with its fangs, injecting venom before letting it go. The snake waits a while for its victim to die, then tracks it down and eats it.

SIZE: 4–6 ft. long (rarely up to 8 ft.)

EGGS: The female gives birth to 15–20 live young on average

FOUND IN: Coastal forests (especially pine and palmetto), scrublands, sandhills, and barrier islands

CAROLINA WREN
(Thryothorus ludovicianus)

Carolina wrens are non-migratory and stay in the same general area year-round. They spend most of their time feeding on the ground, and as a result, many are killed by feral and pet cats that are allowed to roam outdoors.

Like some other wrens, a male Carolina wren will often build multiple nests. The female will select just one of these to lay her eggs in. The reason for the multiple nests isn't fully understood. It might be to help the female assess the male's nest-building skills, or it might also be to fool predators.

SIZE: 5.5 in. long; 7.5 in. wingspan

DIET: A wide range of insects and spiders; also some fruits and seeds, especially in winter

FOUND IN: Open woodlands, suburban yards, and other areas with thickets and brushpiles

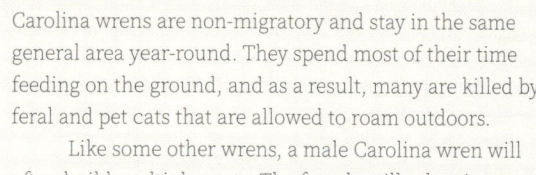

LOGGERHEAD SEA TURTLE
(Caretta caretta)

The loggerhead sea turtle, often just called a "loggerhead," owes its large head to powerful jaw muscles. These help the turtle feed on hard-shelled prey, such as conch, whelks, and crabs.

Female loggerheads lay their eggs in the sand on ocean beaches. They often nest on the same beach as they hatched from themselves, or one very close by. Somehow, they find their way there after decades, and after traveling thousands of ocean miles! When baby loggerheads hatch from their eggs, they dig their way to the surface of the sand, after which they head toward the water to begin their ocean life. If they reach the water, they must survive many predators and dangers to reach adulthood. It takes the female 35 years until she can lay her first set of eggs. It is estimated that only between one in a thousand and one in ten thousand hatchlings survive to adulthood!

SIZE: 2.5–3.5 ft. long

EGGS: The female lays an average of 100–125 eggs underground, in the sand on a nesting beach

FOUND IN: Sandy beaches when first hatched, then the ocean and coastal waters

SOUTH DAKOTA

South Dakota is roughly split down the center by the Missouri River. Elevation generally rises as you go west from the river. The most notable landscape element in South Dakota is the Black Hills, along the state's western border. There are several peaks here that reach just over 7,000 feet.

BLACK HILLS SPRUCE
(Picea glauca)

The Black Hills spruce is the state tree of South Dakota. It is a variety of white spruce, found only in southwestern South Dakota and a small part of northeastern Wyoming. It is the only native spruce in the Black Hills region.

The Black Hills spruce provides great cover for birds in winter. Many birds feed on its seeds, and its bark is eaten by porcupines. Indigenous communities once used it for many purposes, including making chewing gum from its hardened sap. Today, it also has a variety of uses, and is probably best known as a popular Christmas tree.

HEIGHT: 30–50 ft.

FOUND IN: Throughout the Black Hills region

SEASON: Cones drop in the fall

PASQUEFLOWER
(Pulsatilla patens)

In many of the areas where it grows, pasqueflower is one of the first spring flowers to bloom, often even emerging when snow is still on the ground. It grows across an impressive elevational range, and can be found anywhere from 300 to 12,500 feet above sea level.

There is more to pasqueflower plants than just their pretty violet flowers. The entire plant is covered in a large concentration of long, silky hairs. When hit by specific angles of sunlight, this makes it look like it's surrounded by smoke. As a result, it has earned the nickname "prairie smoke."

HEIGHT: 0.5–1.5 ft.

FOUND IN: Prairies, open woodlands, and rocky outcrops

SEASON: Flowers in early spring

PLAINS PRICKLY PEAR
(Opuntia polyacantha)

Plains prickly pear is one of the most cold-tolerant of all cacti. It is found as far north as parts of the Yukon in Canada, where temperatures can be as cold as fifty degrees below zero.

The cactus' spines are modified leaves, and help keep animals from eating the plant. The flowers of plains prickly pear are initially yellow, but as the season goes on, they transition to being more red in color. This is thought to be a strategy to attract different pollinators, which would increase the chances of pollination.

HEIGHT: 4–12 in.

SEASON: Flowers from late spring to early summer; fruits ripen late summer and early fall

FOUND IN: A wide diversity of settings, including sagebrush, open coniferous woodlands and forests, shrublands, and more

AMERICAN LICORICE
(Glycyrrhiza lepidota)

American licorice, or "wild licorice," has a long history of medicinal use by indigenous communities. Teas from its dried leaves or roots were once used to relieve upset stomachs, coughs, chest pain, sore throats, and earaches. The roots were commonly chewed and kept in the mouth to relieve toothache pain.

Parts of the roots of American licorice are up to fifty times sweeter than sugar. Its sweetness comes from a compound named glycyrrhizin. American licorice is not what we use to make our licorice candy. That's a good thing, as glycyrrhizin is known to raise blood pressure.

HEIGHT: 1–3.5 ft.

SEASON: Flowers in summer; fruits ripen late summer to early fall

FOUND IN: Prairies, thickets along streams and rivers, and moist meadows

SOUTH DAKOTA

EASTERN FOX SQUIRREL
(Sciurus niger)

The eastern fox squirrel is the largest native tree squirrel in North America. These are almost twice as large as gray squirrels. Eastern fox squirrels are good climbers. This has a lot to do with their sharp, recurved claws. They often raise their young in tree cavities, which they also use as winter dens, and which provide them with effective shelter from harsh winter weather. During warmer times of year, they make use of stick platforms, which they build high in tree branches.

SIZE: 1.5–2.5 ft. long (tail is half of that length)

FOUND IN: Open woodlands and forests

DIET: A wide range of nuts, seeds, fruits, fungi, and insects

YELLOW-HEADED BLACKBIRD
(Xanthocephalus xanthocephalus)

Yellow-headed blackbirds are a sight to see. Their yellow heads and chests contrast strikingly with their dark brown bodies.

Yellow-headed blackbirds nest in the same wetland habitats as red-winged blackbirds, though in deeper water sections. They are larger than the red-winged variety, and dominant over them.

Because their nests are located in vegetation over the water, nestlings sometimes fall into the water below. When this happens, they often have to swim short distances to get back to the vegetation.

SIZE: 8–10 in. long; 15 in. wingspan

DIET: A wide variety of invertebrates during the warmer months, and mostly seeds and grains in the winter

FOUND IN: Marshes and other wetlands with emergent vegetation such as cattails and rushes

GREAT PLAINS TOAD
(Anaxyrus cognatus)

The Great Plains toad is well adapted to arid environments. During particularly dry and hot conditions, they will often burrow underground. This helps to keep them from drying out and/or overheating. They will sometimes stay in their burrows for over two weeks during these conditions.

Great Plains toads breed in shallow water, usually after heavy spring or summer rainstorms. The males attract females to the wetland with their metallic-sounding trill, which lasts 25–50 seconds and sounds like a high-pitched jackhammer.

SIZE: 2–3.5 in. long

EGGS: The female lays an average of 10,000–12,000 eggs (though sometimes upwards of 20,000)

FOUND IN: Prairies and floodplains

TWELVE-SPOTTED SKIMMER
(Libellula pulchella)

The twelve-spotted skimmer is named because it has twelve brown spots across all of its four wings—three of these spots on each. The male, however, has ten additional white spots, so some people call it the "ten-spotted skimmer."

Twelve-spotted skimmers are very active—particularly the males, which are very territorial. They often fly along the edges of large wetlands to patrol their territory. If they see another male, or even a different type of dragonfly, they will often chase it away.

SIZE: 2 in. long; 2 in. wingspan

EGGS: The female can lay hundreds of eggs per day

FOUND IN: A variety of freshwater wetlands, especially those with emergent vegetation; also open fields, where they feed

Tennessee

Tennessee has a large number of animal and plant species, especially for its size. This is thanks to a wide variety of ecoregions in the state. Tennessee has many different types of forests, a wide range in elevation, and an extensive saltwater coastline. It also has lots of caves and other interesting geological features, which are home to some unique plants and animals.

AMERICAN SYCAMORE
(Platanus occidentalis)

The American sycamore is quite long-lived, especially for a hardwood tree. It often survives at least 200 years, and sometimes upwards of 500. These trees grow quite large and can have very wide trunks. The largest recorded American sycamore had a trunk that was almost 15 feet across.

The inner wood (called the "heartwood") of American sycamores tends to decompose quickly. This often results in large hollow cavities in the tree. Many animals make use of these, including bats, birds, squirrels, and other mammals. Sometimes black bears use the hollows as dens.

HEIGHT: Typically 75–100 ft., but can grow upwards of 150 ft.

FOUND IN: Moist, low-lying areas such as along streams and rivers

SEASON: Flowers in early spring; fruits ripen early fall and drop throughout winter

TENNESSEE PURPLE CONEFLOWER
(Echinacea tennesseensis)

The Tennessee purple coneflower is a type of echinacea plant, from which the herbal supplement is made. It is popular in teas, for example, that boost the immune system to ward off illness. The word "echinacea" comes from the Greek "echinos," which means "hedgehog." This is a reference to the spiky center of the flower.

The Tennessee purple coneflower is only found in the wild in the central part of Tennessee. It was once an endangered species in the U.S. Thanks to the work of many conservation groups, it is now secure. It was removed from the endangered species list in 2011.

HEIGHT: 2–2.5 ft.

SEASON: Blooms throughout the summer

FOUND IN: Limestone cedar glades in the greater Nashville area

CHRISTMAS FERN
(Polystichum acrostichoides)

The Christmas fern is an evergreen fern. It is one of the most common ferns in the eastern United States and got its name from early European colonizers making Christmas wreaths from its branches.

In winter, Christmas ferns tend to lie flat on the ground, compacted by heavy snow, whereas the rest of the year they grow more upright. Fallen leaves often get trapped beneath the compacted ferns, which creates a unique habitat for some forest floor animals. It particularly benefits salamanders, along with many invertebrates, including beetles.

HEIGHT: 1.5–2 ft.

SEASON: Retains leaflets year-round

FOUND IN: Shady, moist areas, typically forests and rocky slopes

STRIPED WINTERGREEN
(Chimaphila maculata)

Striped wintergreen is an evergreen plant, bringing green color to the forest floor during the winter months. Because there are fewer leaves on the canopy above them, these plants benefit from extra sunlight in winter, storing it for use during the summer. A similar plant is the American wintergreen, which can be distinguished by its more minty scent.

HEIGHT: 4–10 in.

SEASON: Blooms in summer, fruits in early fall, and fruits remain on plant throughout winter

FOUND IN: Shady forests, woodlands, and slopes

Tennessee

AMERICAN BLACK BEAR
(Ursus americanus)

The American black bear is one of three bear species in the United States. The other two are the polar bear and the brown bear, of which the grizzly bear is a subspecies.

American black bears spend most of their time feeding. This is especially true from late summer to fall, since they need to gain extra weight to survive the winter. In the northern parts of their range, they often overwinter in dens. These can be in rock crevices, in hollow trees, under the roots of fallen trees, or in brush piles, among other locations. Further south, American black bears are often active throughout the year.

SIZE: 5–6 ft. long

DIET: A wide range of plants, berries, fruits, nuts, corn, insects, and occasionally carrion

FOUND IN: Forests, woodlands, and, increasingly, suburban areas

WILD TURKEY
(Meleagris gallopavo)

Wild turkeys live in flocks, which can sometimes include upwards of a hundred individuals. They spend a lot of daytime hours on the ground feeding, and living in flocks means they can keep as many eyes as possible out for predators. Wild turkeys have very powerful vision—much sharper than ours—and, because their eyes are on the sides of their heads, they have a much wider field of vision than we do.

Wild turkeys roost up in trees at night—another anti-predator strategy. Though fairly bulky, they are actually quite agile fliers.

SIZE: 4 ft. long, 5 ft. wingspan (males); 3 ft. long, 4 ft. wingspan (females)

DIET: Nuts (especially acorns), seeds, grains, berries, and insects

FOUND IN: Areas where forests and woodland abut open areas, such as fields and meadows

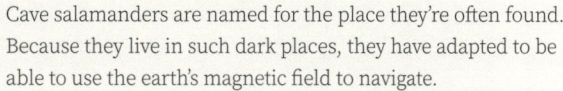

CAVE SALAMANDER
(Eurycea lucifuga)

Cave salamanders are named for the place they're often found. Because they live in such dark places, they have adapted to be able to use the earth's magnetic field to navigate.

Cave salamanders are a bright-orange color, which warns predators that they are toxic. When a potential predator comes close, they coil up their bodies, then wave their tails over their heads to intimidate and scare the predator away.

SIZE: 4–6 in. long

EGGS: The female lays 50–90 eggs in water

FOUND IN: Caves, under rocks and logs, and in rock crevices along rivers and streams

COMMON EASTERN FIREFLY
(Photinus pyralis)

The common eastern firefly is one of over 150 species of fireflies in the United States. Fireflies, or "lightning bugs," produce flashes of light to communicate. This mostly occurs between males and females, as they each look to find and attract a mate.

The common eastern firefly is sometimes called the "big dipper firefly." The male's flashing pattern resembles a "J," which resembles the big dipper constellation. If a female is interested in the male, she will flash back at him.

SIZE: Approx. 0.5 in. long

EGGS: The female lays around 500 eggs in damp soil

FOUND IN: Meadows, fields, and woodland edges

TEXAS

Texas is home to over 6,000 combined species of animals and plants. This ranks second only to California in species diversity among all fifty states. This has much to do with the large size of Texas (it is the second-largest state in the U.S.) and the fact that it is one of the most southerly states. It also has a wide variety of ecoregions, and quite an extensive coastline along the Gulf of Mexico.

PECAN
(Carya illinoinensis)

The pecan is the state tree of Texas, and is best known for the nuts it produces. These nuts are described as having a buttery flavor, and can be eaten fresh or roasted. They're a key ingredient in many different recipes, often sweet treats like pecan pie, cakes, cookies, and ice cream.

Around 270 million pounds of pecan nuts are harvested in the U.S. each year. This represents about half of the world's total pecan harvest.

HEIGHT: Typically 70–100 ft., though sometimes up to 150 ft.

FOUND IN: Areas with high humidity and rich, fertile soils

SEASON: Flowers mid- to late spring. Nuts are ripe and harvested throughout the fall

TEXAS BLUEBONNET
(Lupinus texensis)

The Texas bluebonnet, also commonly known as the "Texas lupine," is the state flower of Texas. The flower gets its name because its petals look like bonnets—hats worn by babies to protect them from the sun.

When in bloom, fields of Texas bluebonnets can provide stunningly beautiful violet-colored vistas. They are so popular that the Texas Department of Transportation seeds many roadsides with them each year. There are a number of annual festivals in Texas that celebrate these flowers.

HEIGHT: 1–2 ft.

FOUND IN: Open areas such as fields, prairies, hillsides, and roadsides

SEASON: Blooms early to mid-spring

PINKLADIES
(Oenothera speciosa)

Pinkladies, also called "pink evening primrose," are different from most flowers in that they primarily bloom at night. During the daytime, when they are hit by full sunlight, the flowers close, though they will sometimes open up on cloudy days.

These flowers have a distinct look, and are often described as pink satellite dishes. Because they are open at night, they are often pollinated by moths. The seed capsules they create are eaten by various birds, particularly finches, as well as some small mammals.

HEIGHT: 1–2 ft. tall

SEASON: Blooms late spring to mid-summer

FOUND IN: Prairies, grasslands, and open woodlands

HONEY MESQUITE
(Prosopis glandulosa)

Honey mesquite grows as a medium-sized shrub or a small tree. Each inflorescence is made up of hundreds of small flowers. These are very fragrant and attract many pollinators, mostly bees, which is where the "honey" part of the name comes from.

The honey mesquite has a long history of use by indigenous communities, who have made medicines and foods from the plant. Its thorns have been used as tattoo needles, for firewood, and for smoking meats over.

HEIGHT: 20–30 ft.

SEASON: Flowers in spring and summer; seedpods ripen in late summer

FOUND IN: Plains and dry rangelands

COYOTE
(Canis latrans)

Coyotes are extremely adaptable, and are able to thrive in most any setting, even in some of the most urban areas. They live as a pack, typically consisting of an adult pair, the pups of the year, and sometimes a helper sibling born the previous year. Females give birth to pups in a den in early spring. Dens might be made in a hollowed-out tree stump or a rocky outcrop, or excavated underground by the coyotes themselves. The pups remain with their parents and siblings until the fall, when they disperse to set up their own territories elsewhere.

SIZE: 2–4 ft. tall

DIET: Small- to medium-sized mammals, reptiles, amphibians, insects, berries, and vegetation

FOUND IN: Almost any setting, including the most rural to the most urban areas, as long as there is some green space

PAINTED BUNTING
(Passerina ciris)

Male painted buntings are one of the most beautiful North American birds. In the 1800s, this beauty sadly resulted in thousands being caught each year to be sold as pets. It is against the law to do this in the U.S. now, but it does still happen in some other countries.

Painted buntings spend much of their time feeding on the ground. They will sometimes even take insects that are caught in spider webs. These birds are very wary when feeding on the ground, pausing frequently to look for predators.

SIZE: 5.5 in. long; 8.5 in. wingspan

DIET: Seeds and insects

FOUND IN: Woodland edges, brushy areas, and roadsides

TEXAS SPINY LIZARD
(Sceloporus olivaceus)

Texas spiny lizards blend in quite well with their environment—typically leaf litter on the ground. They also camouflage well against trees and fences, where they often climb and bask. They are very skittish creatures, wary of potential predators. When approached, they will quickly flee.

Male Texas spiny lizards use various forms of display to show dominance over other males. They might show off with "push-ups," for example, or bob their heads and extend their bright-blue throats. They will use similar displays to attract females as well.

SIZE: 9–11 in. long

EGGS: The female lays an average of 10 eggs up to 4 times per year

FOUND IN: Locations with mesquite trees, mostly, though also in suburban areas with fences and utility poles

TEXAS BROWN TARANTULA
(Aphonopelma hentzi)

The Texas brown tarantula is one of over twenty-five tarantula species in the United States. "Texas browns," as they are often called, are active mainly at night, which they spend mostly hunting. They hunt actively on the ground, mainly for insects, rather than making a web to catch food. They spend the daytime underground in their burrows. Females lay their eggs in their burrows, and will guard them for the one-and-a-half to two months they take to hatch.

Females can be quite long-lived, and can live upwards of thirty years in the wild. Males rarely live more than a year in the wild.

SIZE: 4 in. legspan

EGGS: The female lays up to 1,000 eggs at a time

FOUND IN: Relatively open areas such as scrublands, grasslands, and prairies

Utah

Utah is quite a large and undeveloped state. As a result, it has a substantial number of plant and animal species. At almost 3,900 combined species, this ranks Utah tenth across all fifty states in terms of combined plant and animal biodiversity. It also has quite a range of elevation differences throughout the state. The difference between the lowest and highest points in Utah is just over 11,500 feet!

QUAKING ASPEN
(Populus tremuloides)

Quaking aspen gets its name from the way its leaves flutter, or "quake," in light breezes. The stalks of its leaves, called "petioles," are flattened, which is what makes the leaves flutter as they do. Quaking aspens often grow in massive colonies, and many trees in a given area are clones of one another, sharing a single root system underground. This means they aren't actually individual trees, but rather different stems of the same tree. One of these, in Utah, is the largest known living organism on Earth, and is approximately 80,000 years old! It is made up of almost 50,000 individual stems, which cover over 100 acres and weigh about 6,000 tons. That is equal to the weight of over 1,000 African Elephants! Quaking aspen leaves turn a stunning gold color in the fall. In a colony, they will often all change color at the same time, which makes for an extraordinary sight. People travel a long way to see these beautiful vistas.

HEIGHT: 40–70 ft.

SEASON: Flowers in mid-spring; fruits ripen late spring into summer

FOUND IN: Almost any setting except for areas of permanently wet soil

UTAH JUNIPER
(Juniperus osteosperma)

Utah junipers are hardy trees that can live in quite dry landscapes. As a result, they are one of the most widespread trees in the Great Plains region. Many birds and mammals disperse their seeds. One bird species, the Townsend's solitaire, plays a big role in this, since it eats a lot of juniper berries.

The Utah juniper can live quite long, often over 500 years. The oldest identified to date is over 1,900 years old! Though these trees are long-lived, they don't grow very tall. They do, however, grow in a wide variety of interesting shapes.

HEIGHT: 10–25 ft.

SEASON: Flowers in early spring

FOUND IN: Dry open areas such as plains, plateaus, and lower mountain slopes

SEGO LILY
(Calochortus nuttallii)

The sego lily is the state flower of Utah. All parts of this plant are edible and were a key food source for indigenous communities and early settlers in the state. Anyone considering eating them should be very careful, though. They look very similar to another plant, called "death camas," which is toxic.

When in bloom, each sego lily has a single flower. These are quite beautiful, and add wonderful color to the semidesert areas where they are found. They only bloom for a very short period, though, before quickly drying up.

HEIGHT: 6 in.–1.5 ft.

SEASON: Blooms late spring to early summer

FOUND IN: Grasslands, sagebrush foothills, and high desert areas

Utah

PRONGHORN
(Antilocapra americana)

The pronghorn is the fastest land mammal in the U.S., and the second-fastest in the world. They can reach a maximum speed of between 55 and 60 miles per hour. Only the cheetah is faster, though pronghorns can maintain their top speeds for much longer than cheetahs.

The pronghorn is named for the pair of relatively short horns on top of its head. Both the male and the female have these, though the females' are smaller, typically just a bump. Pronghorns have large eyes and powerful vision, useful for keeping a lookout for predators.

SIZE: 3–5 ft. long; 2.5–3 ft. tall at the shoulder

FOUND IN: Open settings such as grasslands, plains, shrublands, and deserts

DIET: Vegetation, mostly including shrubs and grasses as well as wildflowers, fruits, and other plants

MOUNTAIN BLUEBIRD
(Sialia currucoides)

Male mountain bluebirds are well known for their strikingly beautiful blue plumage. They used to be called the "ultramarine bluebird," because of their deep-sea shade of blue.

Mountain bluebirds feed mostly on insects, which they capture in a variety of ways. Sometimes they feed while standing and hopping on the ground. At other times, they will launch from a perch, such as a branch, and catch the insect(s) in midair before returning to that perch. Sometimes, they hover low over the ground before pouncing on insect prey.

SIZE: 6.5–8 in. long; 11–14 in. wingspan

FOUND IN: Open areas with scattered trees and/or shrubs

DIET: Mostly insects, but also small fruits and seeds in winter

CANYON TREE FROG
(Hyla arenicolor)

Despite their name, canyon tree frogs actually tend to spend much more time on rock faces and boulders than they do in trees. They are very adept climbers, and thanks to their powerfully gripping toepads, are able to climb sheer vertical surfaces like rockfaces.

Canyon tree frogs are mainly active during the nighttime. Due the daytime and/or during times of little rainfall, they often retreat to rock crevices. This gives them a place to stay relatively cool, moist, and safe from predators, as their pattern and coloration camouflages well against the rocks.

SIZE: 2–2.5 in. long

EGGS: The female lays 100 or more eggs in a wetland

FOUND IN: Rocky canyons and nearby streams

TEN-LINED JUNE BEETLE
(Polyphylla decemlineata)

Ten-lined June beetles get their name from the time of year when they emerge—mostly in June or July. They are attracted to lights, both at night and during the daytime.

These beetles often make a hissing sound when touched, which they achieve by pushing their wings down against their bodies. This pushes out air out to create the sound. The male has very large and distinctive antennae, which look somewhat like a set of very long eyelashes. He uses these to the detect the smell signals given off by females, called "pheromones."

SIZE: 1–1.5 in. long

EGGS: The female lays 60–70 eggs underground

FOUND IN: Gardens, croplands, orchards, and open woodlands

VERMONT

Vermont is heavily forested. In fact, it is the sixth most forested state, with seventy-eight percent of its land area being covered by forest. Throughout the state, there is a great diversity of elevation, which is largely the result of glaciation that took place in the region between 10,000 and 25,000 years ago. Vermont is home to some really neat plant and animal species, though the total number is limited by the state's relatively small size, as well as how far north it is.

STAGHORN SUMAC
(Rhus typhina)

Staghorn sumac often grows as a colony, starting as a single stem. Over time, clones emerge outward from the first stem in a somewhat circular pattern. Those that are furthest from the central stem are therefore the youngest.

Staghorn sumac plants grow many forked branches, which have a soft, velvety covering, and look a bit like deer antlers when they are growing. This is where the "staghorn" part of the name comes from.

This plant produces unique red, hairy fruits, which form cone-shaped clusters at the branch tips. Many birds feed on them in the winter.

HEIGHT: 15–30 ft.

SEASON: Flowers in early spring; fruits ripen in late summer and can remain well into winter

FOUND IN: Open fields, woodland edges, and roadsides

RED TRILLIUM
(Trillium erectum)

Red trillium is one of more than thirty-five trillium species found in the United States. The name "trillium" comes from the prefix "tri," which means three. This is because all trilliums have three leaves, and their flowers each have three sepals and three petals.

The red trillium has many other names. Some of these include: "stinking benjamin," "illscented trillium," and "wet dog trillium," thanks to the unpleasant smell that its flowers give off. This strong, unpleasant smell attracts pollinators like carrion beetles and flesh flies.

HEIGHT: 1–1.5 in.

SEASON: Blooms in mid-spring

FOUND IN: Areas of rich, acidic soils in open woodlands

SUGAR MAPLE
(Acer saccharum)

The sugar maple is the official state tree of Vermont, and is so emblematic that it's depicted on the state quarter. Sugar maples are the main source of maple syrup, which is made by placing a tap in each tree to extract the sap.

The sap, which comes out clear, is then boiled, evaporating any water and leaving just syrup behind. It takes an average of about 40 gallons of sap to make 1 gallon of maple syrup! And Vermont produces about half of all of the United States' maple syrup each year.

Sugar maples were widely planted along roadsides during the 1800s because they produce abundant shade, and turn beautiful shades of yellow, orange, and red in the fall. However, many of these trees have died as a result of being very susceptible to pollution and soil acidification (from acid rain), and of being negatively impacted by road salts used for road de-icing.

HEIGHT: 60–75 ft.

FOUND IN: Areas with well-drained soils

SEASON: Flowers in early to mid-spring. Sap is tapped for syrup in late winter

VERMONT

NORTH AMERICAN PORCUPINE
(Erethizon dorsatum)

The North American porcupine is the second-largest rodent in North America, the largest being the American beaver. North American porcupines are famous for their quills, which cover their whole body, except for the belly. Each adult has approximately 30,000 quills, helping keep them safe from many potential predators.

The porcupine's quills are actually modified hair, made from the same protein that our fingernails and toenails are made from. A popular myth is that the porcupine can shoot its quills, but in fact, it merely raises them when threatened, and detaches them if touched.

SIZE: 2–3 ft. long

DIET: A variety of plants, fruits, seeds, and leaves; evergreen needles and the inner bark of trees in winter

FOUND IN: Forested areas with coniferous trees and/or fruit trees

RUBY-THROATED HUMMINGBIRD
(Archilochus colubris)

The ruby-throated hummingbird is found throughout the eastern U.S., and is the only hummingbird that regularly breeds in the region. It's the males that have the bright ruby-colored throat; the females have a mostly white throat, with very modest speckling.

Hummingbirds get their name from the humming sound made by their fast-flapping wings. Ruby-throated hummingbirds beat their wings approximately fifty times per second on average. During some mating displays, they will even beat their wings as fast as 200 times per second. They are also very skilled fliers. They can hover, or fly forward, backward, and sometimes even upside down!

SIZE: 4 in. long; 4.5 in. wingspan

DIET: Nectar, pollen, and insects

FOUND IN: Open areas with nectar-producing flowers that abut deciduous woodlands

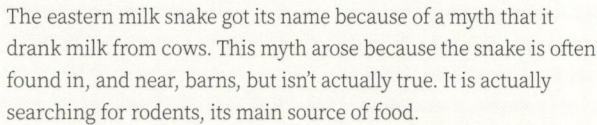

EASTERN MILK SNAKE
(Lampropeltis triangulum)

The eastern milk snake got its name because of a myth that it drank milk from cows. This myth arose because the snake is often found in, and near, barns, but isn't actually true. It is actually searching for rodents, its main source of food.

Unlike most other snakes in Vermont, eastern milk snakes are mostly active at night, since this is when rodents are also most active. They are also unusual among Vermont snakes in that they constrict their prey, wrapping themselves tightly around it.

SIZE: 2–3 ft. long

EGGS: The female lays an average of 8–10 eggs in a given year

FOUND IN: A wide range of settings, as long as they contain rodents

NORTH AMERICAN LUNA MOTH
(Actias luna)

The North American luna moth in most often just referred to as the "luna moth." It is one of the most strikingly beautiful of all moths found in the United States. Its shape and lime-green coloration helps it camouflage with leaves. These moths have quite distinctive, long "tails," extending back from their hindwings. These disrupt the echolocation process of bats who might be hunting them.

Male luna moths have long and feathery looking antennae. They use these to detect pheromones released by females. A male can detect a female from a mile or more away!

SIZE: 3–4.5 in. wingspan

EGGS: The female lays 200–400 eggs

FOUND IN: Deciduous woodlands and forests and surrounding areas

Virginia

Virginia has a relatively large number of plant and animal species for its fairly small size. Though it is only the thirty-sixth largest of all fifty states, it is the twelfth most biodiverse. This is largely the result of it being heavily forested, with quite a diversity in elevation, and the eighth-longest saltwater coastline of all states.

BLACK GUM
(Nyssa sylvatica)

The fruits of black gum trees are very important to migrating birds during the fall, since they ripen earlier in the season than the berries and fruits of many other plants. Their leaves also change color earlier than those of many other trees. This is believed to be a signal to attract birds to the fruits, known as "foliar fruit flagging."

Black gum trees are one of the oldest living trees in the eastern U.S. Some have been found to be more than 600 years old.

HEIGHT: 40–60 ft.

SEASON: Blooms in spring; fruits ripen in early fall

FOUND IN: Wet forests and along wetlands such as swamps, riverbanks, and floodplains

WINTERBERRY
(Ilex verticillata)

Winterberry is a type of holly. It gets its name from the berries that stay on the shrubs all winter, unless birds or other animals eat them first. The bright-red berries provide a burst of color in winter landscapes.

Winterberry is popular for home gardens, since it's particularly wildlife-friendly. In addition to the many birds that eat its berries, various insect pollinators feed on nectar from its flowers. Just be careful if you have a cat or dog, because the berries, as well as all other parts of the plants, are toxic to them.

HEIGHT: 5–15 ft.

SEASON: Blooms late spring/early summer; fruits ripen late summer

FOUND IN: Areas of moist soils, often in wetlands

VIRGINIA CREEPER
(Parthenocissus quinquefolia)

Virginia creeper is a vine in the grape family. It is quite abundant where it is found, and often climbs as high as 50 feet, or even more, up trees and powerline poles. Some people plant it in their yards to grow up walls and the sides of their houses. It also grows, or "creeps," extensively along the ground.

Some people misidentify this plant as poison ivy, but you can easily tell the two apart. Poison ivy has three leaves, whereas Virginia creeper has five.

HEIGHT: 50+ ft. long

SEASON: Flowers in early summer; fruits late summer to mid-fall

FOUND IN: Open woodlands, brushlands, and streambanks and riverbanks

VIRGINIA SPRING BEAUTY
(Claytonia virginica)

Virginia spring beauties are quite small and grow low to the ground. They often grow as a colony, with lots of them close to each other, which creates a beautiful swath of pink, purple, and white when they are in bloom.

These flowers grow a tuber underground, like a mini potato. People have eaten tubers for a long time. They taste like potatoes, but they're sweeter, and are packed with vitamins. You can enjoy them boiled, mashed, roasted, fried, or even raw.

HEIGHT: 6–10 in.

SEASON: Blooms in mid-spring

FOUND IN: Moist deciduous forests, forest edges, and meadows

Virginia

VIRGINIA OPOSSUM
(*Didelphis virginiana*)

The Virginia opossum, or simply "opossum," is the only marsupial found in the United States. Marsupials are mammals that give birth to underdeveloped young—the babies grow and develop further in their mother's pouch.

When they are born, baby opossums are only the size of a jelly bean. They then climb into their mother's pouch, where they stay nursing for the next two months. Once they emerge from the pouch, the mother carries them around on her back quite a bit over the next month.

SIZE: 2–3 ft. long

DIET: Varied, including insects, small mammals, birds and eggs, nuts, seeds, fruit, and carrion

FOUND IN: Almost any setting, from the most rural areas to the most densely human-populated urban areas

PILEATED WOODPECKER
(*Dryocopus pileatus*)

The pileated woodpecker is the largest woodpecker in North America. The ivory-billed woodpecker used to be the largest, but it is thought to have gone extinct.

Pileated woodpeckers drill large, rectangular holes in trees to find carpenter ants, which are their main food source. They also eat other insects and larvae that live inside trees. To capture their insect prey, they use their very long, barbed tongues and sticky saliva. Some small birds, like chickadees, use these holes for nests, or seek shelter in them during bad weather.

SIZE: 1.5 ft. long; 2.5 ft. wingspan

DIET: Insects (mostly carpenter ants), also fruits and nuts

FOUND IN: Mature forests and woodlands

COPPERHEAD
(Agkistrodon contortrix)

The copperhead is a beautiful snake, with colors and patterns that help it blend into leaf litter on the ground. Its young have a yellow or yellowish-green tail tip at birth, which they keep for their first three to four years. They wiggle this tail tip, so that it looks like a caterpillar; they do this to lure in prey that eat caterpillars.

Copperheads are venomous snakes, and use this venom to kill their prey. Even so, this venom isn't as strong as that of many other snakes in the U.S.

SIZE: 2–3 ft. long

EGGS: The female gives birth to an average of 6–8 young in a given year

FOUND IN: Rocky, forested hillsides and wetlands

EASTERN CARPENTER BEE
(Xylocopa virginica)

Eastern carpenter bees look a lot like bumblebees, and are often misidentified as such. They get their name because they tend to nest in wood by digging tunnels in wood piles, standing dead trees, and stumps. Often, several females will live and lay their eggs there. You can also find these bees in decks, outdoor furniture, and similar structures. A great way to find them is to look for the wood shavings that pile up under their tunnels.

SIZE: 0.75–1 in. long

EGGS: The female lays 6–8 eggs

FOUND IN: Woodlands and forests and surrounding areas, including suburban ones

WASHINGTON

Washington is one of the most northerly states in the U.S., which somewhat limits its overall plant and animal diversity. However, the state is quite large, with lots of remote areas, and ranges in elevation from sea level to over 14,000 feet! Over 3,300 combined plant and animal species call Washington home, including some very unique and hardy ones.

WESTERN HEMLOCK
(Tsuga heterophylla)

The western hemlock is the state tree of Washington. It tends to be slow growing, often staying below the shade of a full overhead canopy for decades. When a nearby tree dies and falls, it creates a gap in the canopy. This lets in more light, so the western hemlock can grow much faster. These trees are quite long-lived with some living more than 1,000 years.

Western hemlock is widely used as lumber, particularly in the Pacific Northwest. It is also often used for making paper.

HEIGHT: 150–200 ft. **FOUND IN:** Humid areas

SEASON: Cones open in early to mid-fall

PACIFIC RHODODENDRON
(Rhododendron macrophyllum)

The Pacific rhododendron, or "coast rhododendron," is Washington's state flower. In bloom, it brings vibrant color to the shady forests where it usually thrives. Its deep pink flowers bloom in clusters of ten to twenty, and often remain in bloom for a month or longer.

Pacific rhododendrons have shallow roots and are tolerant of dry conditions. They are often planted along steep roadsides in the Pacific Northwest, which helps with erosion control, as well as adding to the scenery.

HEIGHT: 10–20 ft. **FOUND IN:** Relatively dry forests and forest edges

SEASON: Blooms late spring/early summer

RED HUCKLEBERRY
(Vaccinium parvifolium)

Red huckleberry is a very widespread and abundant shrub in the Pacific Northwest. Many birds and mammals eat its berries. They are also a tasty treat for hikers, and can be used to make jelly, pies, and a variety of other sweet treats. Some people even use these berries as fishing bait, since they look a lot like salmon eggs—a popular fish food.

HEIGHT: 4–12 ft.

SEASON: Flowers in mid-spring; berries ripen late summer

FOUND IN: Moist coniferous forests, wetlands edges, and the interface between the two

WESTERN SKUNK CABBAGE
(Lysichiton americanus)

Western skunk cabbage gives off a strong skunk-like odor, especially when it blooms. This helps it attract its insect pollinators, and ought to put other animals off eating it, but some don't seem to mind the skunky smell! Its leaves are often eaten by deer, as well as American black bears. This is especially true in early spring, right after the bears come out of their dens.

Western skunk cabbage is often called "swamp lantern" thanks to the large, somewhat flame-shaped, bright-yellow central part of the plant. This brings bright color to the otherwise shady swampy areas where it grows.

HEIGHT: 1–3 ft.

SEASON: Blooms in early spring

FOUND IN: Wet, wooded areas such as swamps, wet thickets, stream edges, and in seeps and bogs

WASHINGTON

AMERICAN DIPPER
(Cinclus mexicanus)

The American dipper is quite unique. It is the only truly aquatic songbird in North America, catching much of its food underwater. These birds often dive into rivers and streams, and once underwater they walk upstream, flipping stones as they look for invertebrate prey.

American dippers have an extra set of transparent eyelids, so they can see underwater while still protecting their eyes. They also coat their feathers with oil to keep them waterproof. This layer of feathers is nice and thick, so that the American dipper can stay warm in cold water during the winter.

SIZE: 5–8 in. long; 9 in. wingspan

FOUND IN: Clear, fast-flowing mountain streams

DIET: A wide variety of aquatic invertebrates, as well as some small fish and fish eggs

MOUNTAIN BEAVER
(Aplodontia rufa)

Mountain beavers are also referred to as "boomers," and are actually more closely related to squirrels than beavers. They get the "beaver" part of their name because they chew bark and limbs like beavers do.

Mountain beavers dig burrows underground. They spend much of their time in these, unless they are out gathering food. These burrow systems can be complex, often involving many tunnels. Sometimes, they extend as deep as 10 feet underground.

SIZE: 1 ft. long

DIET: A wide variety of plants and plant material

FOUND IN: Moist forests and damp ravines

WOLVERINE
(Gulo gulo)

The wolverine is the largest terrestrial member of the weasel family in the world. It lives a very solitary life, and often travels upwards of 10 miles per day, mainly in search of food.

Wolverines spend much of their time in high-elevation alpine environments. They are well adapted to living in very snowy landscapes, with wide paws that act like snowshoes to keep them on the surface of deep snow. Their fur is adapted so that frost brushes off it easily, though historically this aspect has made them very attractive to fur hunters.

Female wolverines need deep snow—at least 5 feet deep—as this is where they build dens for giving birth and raising their young. The depth of the snow helps keep their young protected from the cold and predators.

SIZE: 3–3.5 ft. long (including tail)

DIET: Small and medium-sized mammals and birds, carrion, and fruit

FOUND IN: High-elevation areas in mountainous terrain, such as tundra and taiga settings

West Virginia

West Virginia is heavily forested. In fact, with about eighty percent of it being covered in forest, it ranks as the fifth most forested of the fifty states. It has a lot of elevational diversity and interesting geological features, especially the eastern half of the state. And even though it is the tenth smallest state, it is home to a surprising diversity of plants and animals.

COMMON PAWPAW
(Asimina triloba)

The common pawpaw bears a large, tasty fruit, which ripens in late summer and early fall. The fruit looks somewhat like a green potato, and often grows in clusters on the trees. It tastes a bit like banana, with hints of citrus and vanilla.

The common pawpaw is very important to a big butterfly known as the "zebra swallowtail." In many of the places where they're found, it's the only plant that zebra swallowtail caterpillars will eat.

HEIGHT: 15–30 ft.

SEASON: Flowers in early spring; fruits ripen late summer and early fall

FOUND IN: Moist and rich soils in wet or damp areas such as along streams, in floodplains, and in ravines

GREAT LAUREL
(Rhododendron maximum)

Great laurel makes up much of the understory throughout the southern Appalachian Mountains. It often grows on steep slopes, where its roots reduce erosion, and the plant gives shelter to many animals.

Great laurel is evergreen, keeping its leaves year-round. When it gets very cold in winter, the leaves often curl downward into long tubes. This is an adaptation to reduce the impact of cold conditions on the leaves. When temperatures warm up in the spring, the leaves then unfold again.

HEIGHT: 5–30 ft.

SEASON: Flowers throughout summer

FOUND IN: Moist, dense woodlands and forests, steep streambanks, and wooded mountain slopes

VIRGINIA BLUEBELL
(Mertensia virginica)

Virginia bluebells are named from their blue, bell-shaped flowers, which have also been described as trumpet-shaped. This shape draws in long-tongued insects, including butterflies, bumblebees, and hummingbird moths, among others. It also attracts hummingbirds themselves.

Virginia bluebells are a type of spring ephemeral. They only bloom for a few weeks in early spring before the leaves in the canopy above leaf out. This enables them to take in sunlight that wouldn't reach the forest floor later in the spring or in the summer.

HEIGHT: 1.5–2 ft.

SEASON: Flowers in early spring

FOUND IN: Moist woodlands, along streambanks, and in floodplains

YELLOW TROUT LILY
(Erythronium americanum)

Like Virginia bluebells, the yellow trout lily is a spring ephemeral, and also only flowers for a short period of time in early spring.

The yellow trout lily is named for its mottled leaves, which look a lot like the patterns on brook trout. Yellow trout lily often grows in large colonies, some of which are more than 250 years old. During any given year, only a small subset of the plants in a colony will flower.

HEIGHT: 4–8 in.

SEASON: Flowers in early spring

FOUND IN: Rich woodlands, rocky woodlands, and streambanks

West Virginia

AMERICAN CROW
(Corvus brachyrhynchos)

American crows are well known for their intelligence. They can imitate many sounds, including songs from other birds, barking dogs, and car horns. They are one of the few bird species known to use tools. For example, they've been seen using pieces of wood to find insects in small crevices.

Young American crows often stay with their parents for a year or so, helping to care for the next year's young. In the winter, American crows often roost together in large groups at night. These roosts can number in the tens of thousands of individuals.

SIZE: 16–20 in. long

DIET: Invertebrates, amphibians and small reptiles, carrion, birds' eggs, seeds, grains, and fruits

FOUND IN: Almost any setting except for the interior of dense forests

EASTERN SPOTTED SKUNK
(Spilogale putorius)

The eastern spotted skunk is one of five skunk species in the U.S., and one of two spotted skunk species. Spotted skunks are the only skunks that can climb trees.

Like all skunks, the eastern spotted skunk sprays a strong, stinky oil at predators. Sometimes, the skunk does a handstand first, which warns potential predators. It often remains in the handstand position when its sprays, which helps with aim.

SIZE: 14–22 in. long (including tail)

DIET: Insects, small mammals, birds' eggs, amphibians and reptiles, and fruits

FOUND IN: Open areas with adequate cover, including thickets, shrubs, brush, and fencerows

TIMBER RATTLESNAKE
(Crotalus horridus)

The timber rattlesnake is one of the most widely distributed venomous snakes in the eastern United States. Like other rattlesnakes, these have a rattle-like growth at the end of their tail, which they use to warn predators to keep their distance.

Timber rattlesnakes are ambush predators. They stay still as they wait for their prey—usually rodents—often resting their heads on a log. Then they strike very quickly with their fangs and inject venom into the prey, after which they will eat it whole.

SIZE: 3–5 ft. long

YOUNG: The female gives birth to 3–12 live young

FOUND IN: Forests and swamps, especially those abutting rocky slopes

ROSY MAPLE MOTH
(Dryocampa rubicunda)

The rosy maple moth is among the most beautiful of all U.S. moths. The mix of pink and yellow colors, along with the woolly texture of its head, body, and legs, creates a surreal look. This coloration is thought to serve two purposes: One is that the bright colors may trick predators into thinking it is toxic. The other is that this color combo and pattern help it blend in with maple tree seed cases, called "samaras."

SIZE: 1.5–2 in. wingspan

EGGS: The female lays 100–200 eggs, in smaller groups on the underside of leaves

FOUND IN: Deciduous forests and woodlands, and urban and suburban areas

WISCONSIN

Where you are in Wisconsin makes a big difference to the kind of natural environment you'll find yourself in. Northern Wisconsin is heavily forested, whereas the eastern part of the state is largely coastal, along Lake Michigan. Southern Wisconsin has abundant plains and savannas, western Wisconsin has a fair amount of elevational diversity, and the central part of the state is largely sandplains and sandhills.

BUR OAK
(Quercus macrocarpa)

Bur oaks are common throughout much of the Midwest. They are a very hardy tree and can tolerate excessive heat and pollution. Thanks to their thick bark, they are also one of the most fire-resistant oak trees.

Bur oak produces very large acorns, more than twice the size of the acorns of other oaks. These ones have a cap that covers more than half of the nut.

HEIGHT: 60–80 ft.

SEASON: Flowers in mid-spring; acorns drop from late summer through mid-fall

FOUND IN: Moist woodlands, prairies, and stream edges

BLACK RASPBERRY
(Rubus occidentalis)

Many different animals like to eat black raspberries. When in season, they are one of the most popular wild food sources, and humans love them too! Lots of people eat them raw, right from the plant. They are also used to make juices, wines, liqueurs, jelly, pies, and more.

The flowers of the black raspberry attract many different insect pollinators. Lots of small mammals use the plant for protective cover, due to its dense, thorny structure. Birds nest in it too for the same reason. Black raspberry bushes are like a small ecosystem in themselves!

HEIGHT: 3–6 ft.

SEASON: Flowers in late spring; fruits ripen early to mid-summer

FOUND IN: Prairies, wooded thickets, suburban yards, and along roadsides

MARSH MARIGOLD
(Caltha palustris)

The marsh marigold brings a bright splash of yellow to wetland edges when its flowers bloom. This plant thrives in wet and damp places, so it's often planted along streams and rivers to help stabilize the banks. Don't pick their flowers, though! They are important for wildlife, and some people will also break out in a rash after handling them.

These flowers attract a lot of insect pollinators. Some small animals, such as frogs, also like to hide in them—they offer good protective cover from predators.

HEIGHT: 1–1.5 ft.

SEASON: Blooms in early spring

FOUND IN: Wet areas such as marshes, ditches, wet woodlands, fens, and swamps

COMMON SELF-HEAL
(Prunella vulgaris)

Common self-heal earns its name from its long history of medicinal use. It has been, and continues to be, used to treat a wide variety of conditions. These include throat ailments, pain, high blood pressure, diabetes, and more.

Common self-heal grows widely on lawns, and is sometimes considered a weed. It often grows as a dense mat, especially when repeatedly mowed. It serves as a key nectar source for various butterflies, bees, and other invertebrates.

HEIGHT: 1–2 ft.

SEASON: Flowers in late spring through early fall

FOUND IN: Grasslands, fields, meadows, suburban yards, and woodland edges

WISCONSIN

AMERICAN BADGER
(Taxidea taxus)

American badgers spend much of their lives underground in their burrows. Aside from a few mild, sunny days, they spend most of winter here. Even in their more active seasons, they stay in their burrows by day, mostly only coming out at night.

Nighttime is when American badgers do their hunting, mostly for burrowing rodents. This includes ground squirrels, prairie dogs, and gophers. They do this by digging the prey out of their own underground burrows. American badgers are well adapted for digging. The claws on their front feet are long and curved, and those on their back feet are more shovel-like, letting them dig in a range of soil conditions. Their narrow snouts help them reach into tight spaces, as do their strong neck and shoulder muscles. These badgers have an extra set of eyelids, which are transparent. These help protect their eyes from dirt and dust while digging.

SIZE: 2–2.5 ft. long

DIET: Mostly small mammals

FOUND IN: Open areas such as grasslands, shrublands, parks, deserts, and agricultural areas

SANDHILL CRANE
(Grus canadensis)

Sandhill cranes are large, long-legged birds that are impressive fliers. In part due to their large wingspan, they are very skilled at soaring. They can soar for hours at a time while only occasionally flapping their wings. During seasonal migrations, their flocks can reach hundreds of individuals. It's quite a sight!

Sandhill cranes have quite intricate courtship displays. These involve wing-flapping, jumping, and bowing. Sometimes they even involve throwing sticks or plants into the air.

SIZE: 3–4 ft. tall; 6–6.5 ft. wingspan

DIET: Seeds, grains, berries, amphibians, small reptiles, and invertebrates

FOUND IN: Open areas, often near water, such as marshes, bogs, and prairies

SPRING PEEPER
(Pseudacris crucifer)

Though quite small, individual male spring peepers make impressively loud calls. To do this, a male inflates his vocal sac, which extends like a balloon from the throat. He does this to attract females to a mating wetland. When hundreds of males (or more) call from a single wetland it can be almost deafening, sometimes audible from over a mile away.

Spring peepers are related to tree frogs. They have adhesive disks on their toe tips (called "toe pads"). They use these to climb shrubs, trees, and sometimes even the sides of houses.

SIZE: 0.75–1.5 in. long

EGGS: Up to 1,000, laid under vegetation

FOUND IN: A wide range of freshwater wetlands to breed; surrounding shrublands and woodlands/forests the rest of the year

GOLDENROD SOLDIER BEETLE
(Chauliognathus pensylvanicus)

Goldenrod soldier beetles are often quite abundant on goldenrod flowers when in bloom. Rather than harming the plants, however, they help to pollinate them. They also help reduce their predation, since these beetles feed heavily on caterpillars, aphids, and other insects that do harm to goldenrod flowers, along with other plants.

To defend themselves against their own predators, goldenrod soldier beetles emit droplets of a noxious liquid from openings along the sides of their abdomens. This keeps the jumping spiders, as well as various birds, away.

SIZE: 0.5 in. long

EGGS: An unknown number, laid in soil

FOUND IN: Sunny, open areas such as meadows, gardens, fields, and roadsides

Wyoming

Wyoming is large and quite undeveloped, which makes it one of the more wild and remote of all states. Its northern location somewhat limits its plant and animal species diversity, though it still has over 3,000 species in total. It is also home to Yellowstone National Park—one of the best-known and most popular of all National Parks in the U.S.

LODGEPOLE PINE
(Pinus contorta)

Lodgepole pine trees often take up large portions of the forested areas they're found in. For example, more than eighty percent of Yellowstone National Park's forested land is lodgepole pine.

Lodgepole pines are easily killed by fire, since their bark is very thin. They also often grow tightly packed together, which makes it easy for fire to spread through their forests. But fire is still important for lodgepole pines. It helps to kill trees that are infected by insects and/or disease, and also opens their cones, enabling them to release their seeds.

HEIGHT: 60–100 ft.

SEASON: Sheds pollen in late spring; cones mature in the fall

FOUND IN: An extremely wide variety of settings

MONUMENT PLANT
(Frasera speciosa)

Monument plants can be quite long-lived, often living upwards of thirty years, and in high altitudes for more than sixty years. Each plant only flowers once in its lifetime, after which it dies. Some years, many of these plants will flower together at one specific location, such as a single mountain slope. Sometimes thousands of individual plants bloom together—an impressive sight! Scientists are not yet sure what conditions cause these synchronized blooms to happen.

HEIGHT: 5–8 ft.

SEASON: Blooms in summer

FOUND IN: Meadows, open ridgelines, and openings in coniferous forests and woodlands

ASPEN FLEABANE
(Erigeron speciosus)

Aspen fleabane, known as "showy fleabane," creates eye-catching patches of lavender and yellow. Its flowers remain in bloom for several months at a time, and they are loaded with nutritious nectar. As a result, they attract a large number of different insect pollinators. There are also some mammals who feed on this plant, particularly pocket gophers and ground squirrels, but also larger mammals such as mule deer, mountain goats, and even domestic sheep.

HEIGHT: 1–2.5 ft.

SEASON: Blooms early summer to early fall

FOUND IN: Grasslands, meadows, and forest openings

GROUSE WHORTLEBERRY
(Vaccinium scoparium)

Grouse whortleberry, also called "grouse huckleberry," produces very sweet-tasting berries. These are loaded with vitamin C and a number of other important nutrients, including carotene. The berries are enjoyed by hikers and animals alike, and get their name from the various grouse species that like to feed heavily on them. They are also eaten by a number of other birds, including ptarmigans and thrushes. The berries are relatively small and grow individually in low densities, meaning it takes time to pick a decent number of them by hand. Some indigenous communities would use comb-like tools to harvest larger numbers of them more efficiently.

HEIGHT: 6–20 in.

SEASON: Blooms early to mid-summer; fruits ripen late summer to early fall

FOUND IN: Coniferous forests, ravines, and open mountain slopes

Wyoming

AMERICAN BISON
(Bison bison)

The American bison is the largest land mammal in North America. It has a massive head with a thick skull, which in winter it uses like a snowplow. Clearing the snow with its head, the bison is able to reach grass and other plants to eat. Males of the species sometimes charge each other, butting their heads together. They do this to decide who gets to mate with a female.

American bison live in herds. These herds used to be tremendous in size. Before European colonizers arrived, more than 30 million American bison roamed the Great Plains. Sadly, they were massively overhunted by the colonizers, and by 1900, there were only around 1,000 wild American bison remaining. Thanks to protections and reintroduction efforts, there are now about 30,000 bison in North America, though that's still only one thousandth of their historical population size.

SIZE: 9–12 ft. long (males); 7–10 ft. long (females); 5.5–6 ft. tall at shoulder height (males and females)

FOUND IN: Prairies, grasslands, plains, sagebrush areas, and river valleys

DIET: Mostly grasses and herbaceous vegetation

GREATER SHORT-HORNED LIZARD
(Phrynosoma hernandesi)

Greater short-horned lizards have many pointed scales, also called "horns." These scales help keep predators away. If approached by a predator, this lizard will often inflate its body to as much as twice its normal size, and can even squirt blood from its eyes! The blood can travel as far as 3 feet, and contains a chemical that is disgusting to predators like coyotes and wolves.

SIZE: 3–5 in. long

YOUNG: Typically gives birth to 6–18 live young (though it can be up to 40)

FOUND IN: Sagebrush, grasslands, deserts, and sparse arid woodlands and shrublands

PAINTED LADY
(Vanessa cardui)

The painted lady is the most widespread butterfly in the world, found in North America, Central America, Europe, Asia, and Africa.

Painted ladies migrate, though their migrations are somewhat unpredictable. Large numbers of them can appear in an area quite suddenly. This most often happens when they migrate from deserts to other areas, possibly because certain flowers are not in bloom, making less food available.

SIZE: 2–3 in. wingspan

EGGS: Lays 200–500 eggs on leaves

FOUND IN: Almost any type of open habitat where there are flowers to feed from

INDEX

A

ALABAMA,	4
ALASKA,	8
ALBATROSS, LAYSAN,	46
ALLIGATOR, AMERICAN,	75
ANOLE, GREEN,	7
ANT,	6, 22, 53, 121, 141, 143, 186
EASTERN BLACK CARPENTER,	119
ARBUTUS, TRAILING,	85
ARIZONA,	12
ARKANSAS,	16
ARMADILLO, NINE-BANDED,	74
ASPEN, QUAKING,	176
ASTER, NEW ENGLAND,	85

B

BADGER, AMERICAN,	198
BAT,	20, 168, 183
BIG BROWN,	70
TRICOLORED,	34
BAYBERRY, NORTHERN,	157
BEAR,	8, 28, 37, 52, 60, 74, 114, 170
AMERICAN BLACK,	161, 168, 170
GRIZZLY,	10, 107
BEAUTYBERRY, AMERICAN,	16
BEAVER,	82
AMERICAN,	6
MOUNTAIN,	190
BEE,	4, 24, 33, 49, 52, 53, 61, 65, 68, 69, 77, 89, 97, 104, 108, 120, 121, 145, 173, 193, 197
BLACK AND GOLD BUMBLE,	95
BROWN-BELTED BUMBLE,	139
COMMON EASTERN BUMBLE,	31
EASTERN CARPENTER,	187
LIGATED FURROW,	103
BEETLE,	53, 69, 169
AMERICAN BURYING,	159
GOLDENROD SOLDIER,	199
RED MILKWEED,	111
TEN-LINED JUNE,	179
BIRCH,	
AMERICAN WHITE,	116
RIVER,	132
BISON, AMERICAN,	202
BITTERROOT,	105
BLACKBERRY, PENNSYLVANIA,	153
BLACKBIRD,	
RED-WINGED,	70, 166
YELLOW-HEADED,	166
BLUEBELL, VIRGINIA,	193
BLUEBERRY,	
HIGHBUSH,	84
LOWBUSH,	77
SHINY,	37
BLUEBIRD,	30, 37
EASTERN,	102
MOUNTAIN,	178
BLUEBONNET, TEXAS,	172
BLUET, AZURE,	133
BOBCAT,	142
BUFFALOBERRY, SILVER,	137
BULLFROG, AMERICAN,	111
BUNCHBERRY, CANADA,	117
BUNTING, PAINTED,	174
BUTTERFLY,	4, 33, 49, 53, 65, 68, 69, 79, 97, 108, 120, 121, 133, 140, 141, 145, 160, 193, 197
BLUE SWALLOWTAIL (SEE ALSO "PIPEVINE SWALLOWTAIL"),	19
COMMON BUCKEYE,	108, 147
EASTERN TIGER SWALLOWTAIL,	83
KARNER BLUE,	131
MONARCH,	25, 53, 65, 111, 129, 155
PAINTED LADY,	203
PEARL CRESCENT,	55
PIPEVINE SWALLOWTAIL,	19, 71
RED-SPOTTED PURPLE,	71
SPICEBUSH SWALLOWTAIL,	99
WESTERN TIGER SWALLOWTAIL,	151
BUTTERWEED,	101

C

CABBAGE,	
EASTERN SKUNK,	153
WESTERN SKUNK,	189
CACTUS,	114
LOW PRICKY PEAR,	33
PLAINS PRICKLY PEAR,	165
SAGUARO,	12, 13
CALIFORNIA,	20
CANDLENUT TREE,	44
CARDINAL FLOWER,	141
BLUE,	33
CARDINAL, NORTHERN,	29, 58, 93
CATERPILLAR,	
EBONY JEWELWING,	91
VIVID DANCER,	115
WOOLLY BEAR,	87
CEDAR, EASTERN RED,	84
CHERRY, BLACK,	57
CHESTNUT, AMERICAN,	128
CHICKADEE, BLACK-CAPPED,	118
CHIPMUNK,	8, 26, 28, 52, 54, 60, 146
EASTERN,	54
CHOKECHERRY,	109
CHOLLA, TREE,	125
COLORADO,	24
COLUMBINE,	
COLORADO BLUE,	24
RED,	52
COMMON WATERSNAKE,	63
CONEFLOWER,	
TENNESSEE PURPLE,	168
UPRIGHT PRAIRIE,	137
CONNECTICUT,	28
COPPERHEAD,	187
CORALBERRY,	145
COREOPSIS, LANCE-LEAVED,	97
CORMORANT, DOUBLE-CRESTED,	34
COTTONWOOD, EASTERN,	64
COYOTE,	102, 110, 114, 174
CRANE, SANDHILL,	198
CREEPER, VIRGINIA,	185
CROSSVINE,	41
CROW, AMERICAN,	194
CROWNVETCH, PENNGIFT,	152
CYPRESS, BALD,	72, 161

D

DEER,	8, 28, 33, 37, 39, 44, 94, 107, 109, 161
MULE,	12, 25, 126, 201
WHITE-TAILED,	152, 154
DELAWARE,	32
DIPPER, AMERICAN,	190
DOGWOOD,	
FLOWERING,	100
ROUGHLEAF,	64
DOVE, MOURNING,	29, 110
DRAGONFLY,	91
EASTERN PONDHAWK,	59
TWELVE-SPOTTED SKIMMER,	167

E

EAGLE, BALD,	11
EAGLE, GOLDEN,	150
EGRET, GREAT,	98
ELDER, RED-BERRIED,	116
ELDERBERRY, RED,	49
ELK,	8, 50, 94, 106, 109
ELM, AMERICAN,	80
EVENING PRIMROSE, PINK,	173

F

FAIRY SLIPPER,	104
FALCON, PEREGRINE,	122, 150
FERN, CHRISTMAS,	169
FIR, DOUGLAS,	148
FIRE PINK,	17
FIREFLY, COMMON EASTERN,	171
FIREWEED,	8
FISHER,	130
FIVE-LINED SKINK,	71
FLEABANE, ASPEN,	201
FLORIDA,	36
FLYCATCHER, SCISSOR-TAILED,	146
FOX,	16, 29, 37, 52, 110, 161
GRAY,	102
RED,	58
FROG,	15, 43, 197, 199
AMERICAN BULLFROG,	111
CANYON TREE FROG,	179
GREEN TREE FROG,	99
PINE BARRENS TREE FROG,	122
SPRING PEEPER,	199
WOOD,	11

G

GEORGIA,	40
GERANIUM, STICKY,	49
GHOST PIPE,	89
GILA MONSTER,	15
GOLDENROD,	199
NORTHERN SEASIDE,	129
TALL,	68
GOLDFINCH, AMERICAN,	54, 145
GOOSE, CANADA,	90
GRAPE,	
MUSCADINE,	161
RIVERBANK,	93
GRAPE, OREGON,	149
GRASHOPPER,	
EASTERN LUBBER,	7
RAINBOW,	127
GROUSE, GREATER SAGE-,	113, 114
GUM, BLACK,	184

H

HACKBERRY, COMMON,	140
HARE,	9, 94
SNOWSHOE,	78
HARVESTMAN, EASTERN,	35
HAWAII,	44
HAWAIIAN GOOSE,	46
HAWK, RED-TAILED,	26
HEMLOCK,	148
EASTERN,	152
WESTERN,	188
HERON	
GREAT BLUE,	134
GREEN,	42
HIBISCUS, YELLOW HAWAIIAN,	44
HICKORY, SHAGBARK,	52
HOLLY	
AMERICAN,	32
POSSUMHAW,	17
YAUPON,	96
HONEY LOCUST,	108
HONEYSUCKLE, CORAL,	160
HUCKLEBERRY, RED,	189
HUMMINGBIRD,	33, 41, 49, 52, 61, 65, 77, 79, 120, 125, 126, 141, 160, 193
RUBY-THROATED,	57, 108, 182
RUFOUS,	50
HYDRANGEA, OAKLEAF,	4

I

IDAHO,	48
ILLINOIS,	52
INDIANA,	56
IOWA,	60
IRIS, DWARF LAKE,	88

J

JACK-IN-THE-PULPIT,	56
JAY, BLUE,	158
JEWELWEED, COMMON,	93
JEWELWING, EBONY,	91
JOE-PYE WEED, SPOTTED,	89
JUNIPER, UTAH,	177

K

KANSAS,	64
KENTUCKY,	68

L

LADY BEETLE, CONVERGENT,	27
LAUREL,	
GREAT,	192
MOUNTAIN,	28
SHEEP,	76
LICORICE, AMERICAN,	165
LILY,	6
CAROLINA,	133
SEGO,	177
YELLOW TROUT,	193
LIZARD,	14, 15, 126
EASTERN COLLARED,	147
FIVE-LINED SKINK,	71
GILA MONSTER,	15
GREATER SHORT-HORNED,	203
TEXAS SPINY,	175
WESTERN FENCE,	51
LOBELIA, GREAT BLUE,	33
LOON, COMMON,	95
LOUISIANA,	72
LUPINE, LARGE-LEAVED,	77

M

MAGNOLIA, SOUTHERN, 96
MAGPIE, BLACK-BILLED, 106
MAINE, 76
MALLARD, 63
MANATEE, WEST INDIAN, 38
MAPLE, 195
    RED, 16, 156
    SUGAR, 181
MARIGOLD, MARSH, 197
MARMOT, YELLOW-BELLIED, 150
MARTEN, AMERICAN, 90
MARYLAND, 80
MASSACHUSETTS, 84
MAYAPPLE, 61
MEADOWLARK, WESTERN, 66
MESQUITE,
    HONEY, 173
    VELVET, 12
MICHIGAN, 88
MILKWEED, 54, 155
    BUTTERFLY, 65
    COMMON, 111, 53
    SHOWY, 25
MINNESOTA, 92
MISSISSIPPI, 96
MISSOURI, 100
MISTLETOE, AMERICAN, 144
MOCKINGBIRD, NORTHERN, 18, 29
MOLE, STAR-NOSED, 158
MONTANA, 104
MONUMENT PLANT, 200
MOOSE, 94, 109, 118, 153
MORNING GLORY, BEACH, 45
MOSS, SPANISH, 161
MOTH, 24, 57, 61, 65, 70, 145, 193
    HUMMINGBIRD CLEARWING, 61, 79
    NORTH AMERICAN LUNA, 183
    ROSY MAPLE, 195
MUSKOX, 9, 10
MUSKRAT, 37, 82

N

NEBRASKA, 108
NEVADA, 112
NEW HAMPSHIRE, 116
NEW JERSEY, 120
NEW MEXICO, 124
NEW YORK, 128
NEWT,
    EASTERN, 131
    ROUGH-SKINNED, 151
NORTH CAROLINA, 132
NORTH DAKOTA, 136

O

OAK, 22
    BLACKJACK, 144
    BUR, 196
    GAMBEL, 124
    NORTHERN RED, 120
    SOUTHERN LIVE, 40, 161
    WHITE, 28
'ŌHELO 'AI, 45
OHIO, 140
OKLAHOMA, 144
OPOSSUM, 16, 17, 29, 142
    VIRGINIA, 186
ORANGE, 36
ORCHID, SHOWY, 81
OREGON, 148
ORIOLE, BALTIMORE, 82
OSPREY, 43
OTTER
    NORTH AMERICAN RIVER, 42
    SEA, 10
OWL, 43, 110, 130, 148
    BARRED, 130

P

PAINTBRUSH, WHOLELEAF, 125
PALM, SABAL, 36
PALMETTO, SAW, 160
PALO VERDE, BLUE, 12
PANTHER, FLORIDA, 39
PASSIONFLOWER, PURPLE, 5
PAWPAW, COMMON, 192
PEA, BEACH, 157
PEACH TREE, 40
PECAN, 172
PEEPER, SPRING, 199
PELICAN, BROWN, 74
PENNSYLVANIA, 152
PEPPERBUSH, SWEET, 120
PEPPERVINE, 73
PERSIMMON, AMERICAN, 100
PHLOX, WILD BLUE, 61
PICKERELWEED, 37

PIKA, AMERICAN, 26
PINE,
    EASTERN WHITE, 76
    GREAT BASIN BRISTLECONE, 112
    JACK, 88
    LOBLOLLY, 16
    LODGEPOLE, 200
    LONGLEAF, 4
    PONDEROSA, 104
    RED, 92
    WESTERN WHITE, 48
PINK LADY'S SLIPPER, 92
PINKLADIES, 173
PINYON, SINGLE-LEAF, 113
PITCHER PLANT
    PALE, 73
    PURPLE, 117
POKEWEED, AMERICAN, 29
POPLAR, YELLOW, 68
POPPY
    CALIFORNIA, 21
    THISTLE, 109
PORCUPINE, 8, 152, 164
    NORTH AMERICAN, 182
PRAIRIE DOG, BLACK-TAILED, 110
PRONGHORN, 25, 178
PUFFIN, ATLANTIC, 78

R

RABBIT, 25, 33, 43, 78, 94, 109, 110, 142, 161
    BLACK-TAILED JACKRABBIT, 14
    EASTERN COTTONTAIL, 66
    SWAMP, 98
RABBITBRUSH, RUBBER, 25
RACCOON, 16, 29, 37, 39, 52, 60, 153, 154
    COMMON, 62
RASPBERRY, BLACK, 196
RATTLESNAKE, PRAIRIE, 27
RATTLESNAKE, TIMBER, 195
REDBUD, EASTERN, 80
REDCEDAR, WESTERN, 48
REDWOOD, COAST, 20
RHODE ISLAND, 156
RHODODENDRON, PACIFIC, 188
ROADRUNNER, GREATER, 126
ROBIN, AMERICAN, 32, 86
ROSE,

S

SAGE, LYRELEAF, 72
SAGEBRUSH, 112
SALAMANDER, 23, 169
    CAVE, 171
    EASTERN RED-BACKED, 91
    EASTERN TIGER, 55
    HELLBENDER, 143
    MARBLED, 135
    SOUTHERN TWO-LINED, 59
    SPOTTED, 119
SALMONBERRY, 9
SASSAFRAS, 156
SCORPION, GIANT DESERT HAIRY, 15
SEA LION, STELLER, 22
SELF-HEAL, COMMON, 197
SEQUOIA, GIANT, 21
SHEEP, BIGHORN, 12, 114
SIDEWINDER, 23
SKUNK, 58, 142
    EASTERN SPOTTED, 194
    STRIPED, 122
SLUG, PACIFIC BANANA, 23
SNAKE, 15, 23, 26, 110, 126, 142
    COMMON WATERSNAKE, 63
    COPPERHEAD, 187
    EASTERN DIAMONDBACK RATTLESNAKE, 162
    EASTERN GARTER, 87
    EASTERN HOGNOSE, 159
    EASTERN INDIGO, 39
    EASTERN MILK, 183
    PRAIRIE RATTLESNAKE, 27
    RING-NECKED, 67
    SIDEWINDER, 23
    TIMBER RATTLESNAKE, 195
SNAKEROOT, WHITE, 129
SOUTH CAROLINA, 160
SOUTH DAKOTA, 164
SPARKLEBERRY, 41
SPICEBUSH, NORTHERN, 29
SPIDER, 15, 35, 50, 99
    BOLD JUMPING, 51
    TEXAS BROWN TARANTULA, 175
    YELLOW GARDEN, 67
SPRING BEAUTY, VIRGINIA, 185
SPRUCE,
    PRICKLY WILD, 60
    WILD PRAIRIE, 136
    COLORADO BLUE, 24
    SITKA, 8
    BLACK HILLS, 164
SQUIRREL, 8, 26, 28, 37, 52, 60, 102, 107, 142, 146, 161, 168, 190, 201
    AMERICAN RED, 30
    EASTERN FOX, 166
    EASTERN GRAY, 18
    SOUTHERN FLYING, 134
    THIRTEEN-LINED GROUND, 138
STONECROP, WOODLAND, 69
STRAWBERRY BUSH, 5
SUMAC, STAGHORN, 180
SUNDEW, PINK, 97
SUNFLOWER, COMMON, 65
SUSAN, BLACK-EYED, 81
SWEETGUM, AMERICAN, 32
SYCAMORE, AMERICAN, 168

T

TARANTULA, TEXAS BROWN, 175
TEAL, BLUE-WINGED, 138
TENNESSEE, 168
TERRAPIN, DIAMONDBACK, 83
TEXAS, 172
THIMBLEBERRY, 105
THISTLE, TALL, 145
TOAD, 43
    EASTERN SPADEFOOT, 35
    GREAT PLAINS, 167
    NEW MEXICO SPADEFOOT, 127
    WESTERN, 106
TORTOISE, 19
    DESERT, 115
    GOPHER, 39, 43
TREE FROG, CANYON, 179
TREE FROG, GREEN, 99
TREE FROG, PINE BARRENS, 122
TRILLIUM,
    GREAT WHITE, 141
    PACIFIC, 149
    RED, 180
TRUMPET VINE, AMERICAN, 57
TULIP TREE, 68
TURKEY, 28, 37, 52, 60, 109, 152
    WILD, 76, 170
TURTLE,
    ALLIGATOR SNAPPING, 30
    COMMON BOX, 61, 154
    GREEN SEA, 47
    LOGGERHEAD SEA, 163
    PAINTED, 139
    RED-EARED SLIDER, 103
    SNAPPING, 30
    THREE-TOED BOX, 19
    WOOD, 79

U

UTAH, 176

V

VERMONT, 180
VERVAIN, HOARY, 108
VIBURNUM, MAPLELEAF, 132
VIOLET, COMMON BLUE, 121
VIRGINIA, 184

W

WALKINGSTICK, NORTHERN, 143
WALNUT, EASTERN BLACK, 60
WASHINGTON, 188
WEASEL,
    FISHER, 130
    LONG-TAILED, 146
WEST VIRGINIA, 192
WHORTLEBERRY, GROUSE, 201
WILLOW, ARCTIC, 9
WINTERBERRY, 184
WINTERGREEN,
    AMERICAN, 121
    STRIPED, 169
WISCONSIN, 196
WOLF, GRAY, 94
WOLVERINE, 191
WOOD-SORREL, VIOLET, 101
WOODCHUCK, 58, 86
WOODPECKER,
    ACORN, 22
    NORTHERN FLICKER, 6
    PILEATED, 186
WREN, CACTUS, 14
WREN, CAROLINA, 162
WYOMING, 200

Y

YARROW, 69
YUCCA, SOAPTREE, 124

To all those who nurture the curiosity and wonder about the natural
world that are innate in all of us—kids and adults alike—B.T.

To my darling husband Michael, who unfailingly indulges me in
my tedious but enthusiastic nature discoveries.—J.D.H.

To my supportive uncle Christian, who shares
my enthusiasm for wildlife and beautiful books. —M.S.A.

America is Wild © 2026 Quarto Publishing plc. Text © 2026 Brad Timm.
Illustrations © 2026 Jill De Haan and Margaux Samson Abadie

First Published in 2026 by Wide Eyed Editions,
an imprint of The Quarto Group.
100 Cummings Center, Suite 265D, Beverly, MA 01915, USA.
T (978) 282-9590 F (978) 283-2742 www.Quarto.com

The right of Jill De Haan and Margaux Samson Abadie to be identified as the illustrators and Brad Timm to be identified as the author of this work has been asserted by them in accordance with the Copyright, Designs and Patents Act, 1988 (United Kingdom).

All rights reserved.

No part of this publication may be reproduced, stored in a retrieval system, or transmitted, in any form, or by any means, electrical, mechanical, photocopying, recording or otherwise without the prior written permission of the publisher or a licence permitting restricted copying.

ISBN 978-1-83600-298-7

The illustrations were created digitally
Set in Bourton and Source Serif Pro

Designer: Myrto Dimitrakoulia
Editor: Amber Husain
Production Controller: Robin Boothroyd
Editorial Director (Commissioning): Lucy Brownridge
Art Director: Karissa Santos
Publisher: Debbie Foy

Manufactured in Guangdong, China TT112025

9 8 7 6 5 4 3 2 1